IP Law for Non-IP Attorneys

Tom James

ISBN: 978-1-946397-09-6

CONTENTS

1 INTELLECTUAL PROPERTY

Intellectual property (IP) is an umbrella term for any output of the human mind as to which a legally enforceable right of ownership exists.

As should be apparent from this definition, not all of the products of a human mind are intellectual property. Writing down memorized facts found in an almanac, for example, involves the generation of output (in this case, the repetition of memorized facts). Mental operations are involved in the generation of such output, but a legally enforceable right of ownership of those facts does not arise as a result of the mental acts of rote memorization and repetition. Property rights in intellectual output arise if and only to the extent that a law in the applicable jurisdiction says they do.

Ideas and expression are the two kinds of output of the human mind that laws in most jurisdictions protect. The bulk of intellectual property law is concerned with defining the particular kinds of ideas and expression in which ownership rights can be claimed and enforced, and under what circumstances.

Intellectual property rights are analogous to tangible property ownership rights, but are not exactly the same. The right of exclusive possession is central to tangible property ownership. The right of exclusive use is the core property right that intellectual property law protects.

Intellectual property must be distinguished from the tangible object in which it is embodied. An intellectual property right in an idea or expression can continue to exist even if all physical embodiments of it have been destroyed.

Kinds

The four principal kinds of intellectual property and the interests they protect are:

- Copyright — expression
- Trademark — source identifiers of products and services
- Patent — inventions
- Trade secret — commercially valuable secret information

This is not an exhaustive list. Examples of other kinds of intellectual property:

- Mask works in semiconductor chips
- Vessel hull designs
- Proprietary information
- Attribution and integrity rights of certain visual artists (aka "moral rights").

Some people classify personality rights (the exclusive right to commercially exploit one's own name, voice or likeness) as a category of intellectual property. Also known as publicity rights, they certainly are intangible property rights. Except in the rare instance where an individual chooses his or her own name, however, a person's name, voice and physical features are more properly regarded as products of the operation of genetics and the choices of an individual's parents and ancestors, not as products of the individual's mind.

The primary emphasis of this publication is on copyrights and trademarks. Patent law is a highly specialized field. In addition to a law license, lawyers wishing to represent clients before the United States Patent Office must demonstrate the requisite level of science/engineering education or training and pass a patent bar examination.[1] Moreover, it is not uncommon for a non-IP attorney to retire from a long career in the law without ever having had to deal with a mask work, trade secret, or vessel hull design. A non-IP attorney is far more likely to encounter copyright and trademark issues.

---

[1] *See* 37 CFR §§ 11.5, 11.6, 11.7, 11.8, 11.9, and 11.16.

Sources of law

Copyrights and patents are governed by federal law. Congressional authority to regulate them derives from Article I, Section 8, clause 8 of the U.S. Constitution. The Copyright Act is the primary source of copyright law. In the 1976 Act, Congress expressly preempted the field. There is no state law of copyright.

Trademarks are regulated by both federal and state law. Congress's concurrent power to regulate trademarks derives from the Commerce Clause. The Lanham Act is the principal federal law regulating trademarks.

Trade secrets are primarily regulated by state law.

Caveats

This book presents a broad overview of U.S. intellectual property law. It does not cover everything there is to know. It is not a substitute for legal research tailored to a client's particular situation and needs. Intellectual property laws change rapidly; no guarantee is made that the information in this book will be current at the time you acquire it. Do not use this book as a substitute for consulting an attorney for legal advice.

Unless the context otherwise requires, references to "he," "him," "she," "her," "s/he," "they," and "them" include persons of any or no gender, and can be used interchangeably.

2 COPYRIGHTS

Requirements

A copyright comes into existence when protectable subject matter is:

a) creative;
b) original;
c) human-created;
d) expressive; and
e) fixed in a tangible medium of expression.

Protection exists for any works that satisfy all of these criteria, whether they are fiction, nonfiction, poetry, plays, screenplays, drawings, paintings, graphic art, photographs, sculpture, architecture, music, sound recordings, motion pictures, audiovisual works, pantomimes, choreography, or computer programs.

Copyright protection does not depend on artistic merit, commercial value, purpose, intended use, or publication. Even email messages and doodles may be protected by copyright.

Neither registration nor a copyright notice is essential to a copyright's existence. At one time, omitting the copyright notice could result in loss of copyright protection, but works published on or after March 1, 1989 are protected by copyright whether copyright notices appear on them or not. There are good reasons to register copyrights and display copyright notices, but liability for copyright infringement may be incurred even if a work is not registered and has no copyright notice on it at the time of the infringement.

Protectable subject matter

To be protected by copyright, a work must be in one of the eight categories specified in the Copyright Act:

- Literary works
- Musical works (including lyrics)
- Dramatic works (including musical accompaniment)
- Pantomime and choreography
- Pictorial, graphic, and sculptural works
- Motion pictures and audiovisual works
- Sound recordings
- Architectural works.

SOUND RECORDINGS

Federal copyright protection for sound recordings first came into existence on February 15, 1972. Before then, the performance and production elements of a sound recording were not protected by federal copyright law even if the owner of the copyright in the underlying work authorized the making of the recording. When Congress amended the Copyright Act to provide copyright protection for sound recordings, sound recordings made before February 15, 1972 did not receive federal copyright protection. Recordings made on or after February 15, 1972 do. The musical or literary works performed on sound recordings, on the other hand, were protected by copyright both before and after 1972. Unauthorized copying of a pre-1972 recording did not infringe a federal copyright in the sound recording, but it could infringe the copyright in the musical composition and/or the lyrics.

Although the 1976 Copyright Act expressly preempted state copyright laws, Congress provided that the preemption of state laws protecting exclusive rights in sound recordings would not go into effect until February 15, 2067. Consequently, sound recordings that were made before February 15, 1972 continued to be protected by state intellectual property laws notwithstanding Congress's declaration of an intention to preempt the field.

The Music Modernization Act 2018 established some federal protections for the owners of rights in sound recordings that were made before February 15, 1972. Pursuant to this Act, federal remedies for unauthorized use of pre-1972 sound recordings are available for 95 years after first publication of the recording, subject to certain additional periods. These periods provide varying additional protection for pre-1972 sound recordings based on when the sound recording was first published. For recordings first published before 1923, the additional time period ended on December 31, 2021. For recordings first published between 1923 and 1946, the additional time period is 5 years after the general 95-year term. For recordings first published between 1947 and 1956, the additional time period is 15 years after the general 95-year term. For all other recordings first fixed prior to February 15, 1972, the additional transition period will end on February 15, 2067.

Some countries began protecting copyrights in sound recordings before the United States did. Sound recordings made in foreign countries may be protected by the copyright laws of those countries irrespective of when the United States began protecting copyrights in sound recordings.

People performing an authorized fixation of a work in a tangible medium may acquire copyright interests of their own if they contribute at least a modicum of creative content. For this reason, a recording artist may acquire a copyright in her authorized performance of a musical work on a recording, and the producer of the authorized recording may acquire a copyright in the production component of the sound recording. A composer may have a copyright interest in the musical work even if the recording is the only medium in which it has ever been fixed. The composer does not lose his copyright in the musical work merely because others have copyright interests in the recording. A copyright in a sound recording of a musical or literary work is separate and distinct from the copyright in the musical or literary work.

A sound recording of a performance of a musical or literary work is a derivative work. Because the owner of the copyright in a work has the exclusive right to make derivative works of it, the owner of the copyright in a musical or literary work has the exclusive right to make sound recordings of it. This right may be licensed to others.

ARCHITECTURE

Copyright protection for architectural designs came into being on December 1, 1990. Both the design for a building (the form, arrangement and composition of spaces) and a depiction of it (blueprint, model or the actual building itself) may receive copyright protection if the building was constructed after November 30, 1990. The design must be fixed in a tangible medium, such as blueprints. The building itself, once constructed, also serves to fix the design in a tangible medium.

Architectural designs that were created before December 1, 1990 do not receive copyright protection if they were published before December 1, 1990, or if they are embodied in a building that was completed before December 1, 1990. An architectural design that was created before December 1, 1990, but was neither published before December 1, 1990 nor embodied in a completed building as of November 30, 1990 is protected by copyright only if a building embodying the design was completed by December 31, 2002. Copyright protection for architectural designs created before, and not published before December 1, 1990, terminated on December 31, 2002 if a building embodying the design had not been completed by then.

Designs for bridges, dams, roads and the like are not protected.

Architectural designs are an exception to the general rule that copyright does not protect utilitarian aspects of a work. Some utilitarian elements of an architectural design receive copyright protection. Standard functional features of buildings (doors, windows, etc.), however, do not. Standard configurations are not protected, either.

A drawing with an architectural design in it may qualify for copyright protection even if the design does not. Unless a drawing qualifies for protection as an architectural work, however, only the expressive aspects of the drawing receive protection; the idea for the design of the building does not.

Since a building is a medium for the expression of its architectural design, it would seem as if photographing or drawing a picture of a building without permission would infringe a copyright in the architectural design. Congress, however, has created an exemption from copyright infringement liability for photographs and drawings of a building if the building is visible to the public. Copying someone else's photograph or drawing of a building might result in liability for infringement of the copyright in the photograph or drawing, but not for infringement of the copyright in the architecture. The exemption does not extend to the making of three-dimensional models or replicas of buildings.

The Copyright Act allows the owner of a building in which architecture is embodied to make or authorize the making of alterations to the building without incurring liability for creating an unauthorized derivative work.

Interior design is not protected by copyright. A work (such as a painting) within it may be protected by copyright, however.

Fixation in a tangible medium

To receive copyright protection, a work must be fixed in a tangible medium of expression.

Although copyright protection does not arise until expression is fixed in a tangible medium, it is the expression, not the medium, which copyright law protects. Once it has been fixed in a tangible medium, copyright protection for the expression continues to exist even if all tangible copies of it are destroyed.

The act of fixing a work in a tangible medium is necessary to the establishment of a protectable copyright, but it is not sufficient. The person who performs the physical act of fixing a work in a tangible medium of expression does not thereby become the owner of the copyright. The creator of expressive content may retain copyright ownership of the content even if he hires or directs another person to perform the act of fixation for him.

THOUGHTS

Thoughts are not protected by copyright until they are fixed in a tangible medium of expression. Copyright protection is not retroactive to the date of the thought.

LIVE PERFORMANCES AND BROADCASTS

Live performances and broadcasts, extemporaneous speech, unscripted dramatic performances, and musical or comedy improvisation are not protected by copyright unless transcribed or recorded in a tangible medium of expression of some kind. Under the Copyright Act definition of fixation, however, a work consisting of sounds and/or images that are transmitted at the time an authorized recording of them is simultaneously being made is considered "fixed" at the time of transmission. Put another way, if a performance is fixed in a tangible medium by means of simultaneously recording it, then copyright protection commences from the time the recording of the performance began, not from the time it is completed. If a band has hired someone to record their concert, then copyright protection begins when the 'Record' switch is flipped and the band begins performing. Consequently, if both an authorized and an unauthorized recording of a performance are made at the time of the performance, the unauthorized recording is an infringement of the copyright in the authorized recording.

A *bootleg recording* is one that is created by recording a live performance without permission. If the performance is of a musical work that is protected by copyright, then the recording would be an infringing derivative work of the musical work. If no authorized recording of the performance is being made at the time the unauthorized recording is, then under ordinary copyright principles, the maker of the bootleg recording would only be infringing the copyright in the musical work, not the copyright in the performance. This is because a copyright in a performance does not exist until an authorized recording of it has begun. Congress has enacted a special statute to deal with this situation. The Anti-Bootlegging Act[2] (part of the Uruguay Round Agreements Act) declares that anyone who makes, transmits, distributes or reproduces an unauthorized recording of a live musical performance is subject to the same liabilities and criminal penalties as a copyright infringer even if the recording does not actually infringe a copyright in the performance.

Expression

Copyright only protects expression. It does not protect information, theories or ideas. The selection and arrangement of information and ideas may be protected by copyright, however, even if the information and ideas are not.

FACTS AND IDEAS

Facts and ideas are not protected by copyright, even when they are fixed in a tangible medium of expression. Thus, while the words used to flesh out a plot may be protected by copyright, the plot of a story is not.

---

2 Pub. L. 103–465, tit. V, §§ 512, 513, 108 Stat. 4809 (codified as amended at 17 U.S.C. § 1101 and 18 U.S.C. § 2319A (2006))

Drawings and diagrams receive copyright protection only for the original artwork and text in them, not the ideas or discoveries they illustrate. An idea for a new game or videogame, the method and procedure for playing the game, and the rules of the game, are not protected by copyright. The text, images, music, sound recordings and/or audiovisual works that are displayed or performed in the course of the game, and any textual matter describing the game, may be protected by copyright, though.

Algorithms, ingredient lists for recipes, blank forms, systems, methods, and processes are all examples of things that do not receive copyright protection because they are ideas.

Because an invention is an idea, it does not receive copyright protection no matter how creative or original it is. A person may have a copyright in the particular words used to describe an invention, but not in the idea or invention itself.

Architectural designs are an exception to the rule that ideas do not receive copyright protection. Sometimes the design of a building may be protected by copyright.

Themes and Moods

The overall theme, mood or message of a work is not protected by copyright.

Utilitarian Features

Because they represent ideas, the utilitarian features of a work (such as a computer program or a sculpture) generally are not protected by copyright. Architectural works are an exception to this rule.

Fonts, Typefaces, and Calligraphy

Fonts, typefaces, calligraphy and typographic ornamentation generally do not receive copyright protection, no matter how novel or creative they may be. This is because the creative aspect of the character usually cannot be separated from its utilitarian function. On the other hand, if it is possible to separate the pictorial or graphic elements from the utilitarian aspects in a particular case, then the decorative elements may receive copyright protection.

MEDICAL, SCIENTIFIC AND TECHNICAL IMAGING

Medical, scientific and technical images—X-rays, MRIs, mammograms, echocardiography, ultrasound, land surveys generated by echo-sounders, etc.—generally are not protected by copyright. They are utilitarian images and communicate only facts and ideas. Just as a copyright claim may be made in a compilation of data, though, so too a copyright claim may be made in the selection and arrangement of a compilation of medical, scientific or technical images. Also, a work created with one of these technologies may receive copyright protection if it is put to an expressive use, such as the creation of modern art.

COMPUTER PROGRAMS

Because ideas are not protected by copyright, only the literal components of a computer program receive copyright protection. The nonliteral aspects (the algorithm, the functions performed, the systems and methods used) do not.

Some courts have held that the sequence, structure and organization (SSO) of a program are protected by copyright. Other courts disagree. The modern trend is to avoid any per se classification of SSO, and to evaluate SSO on a case-by-case basis to determine whether it is an idea, method or process, on one hand, or nonutilitarian expression, on the other.

The source and object code receive copyright protection as literary work. The same general rules apply.

Subject vs. Depiction

Unless the scene or subject of a photograph or drawing is itself a copyrighted work, the subject of a photograph is not protected by copyright.

Merged expression

To the extent a work of authorship does nothing more than communicate factual information or an idea, it is not protected by copyright. In these cases, the idea or fact is said to be *merged* with its expression.

Contest rules are an example. They do not receive copyright protection because the idea (the set of rules) is not separable from the expression of the idea.

Any nonfunctional matter that is not essential to the expression of the idea does not merge. It may be protected by copyright. Illustrations or examples inserted into a set of contest rules in order to help readers understand them better are not necessary elements of the expression of the idea, so they do not merge. They may be protected by copyright.

The more "bare bones" the expression of an idea or information is, the more likely it is that the expression of the idea or information is merged with the idea or information itself, and therefore not protected by copyright.

Creativity

Although copyright law, unlike patent law, does not require an author to demonstrate the creation of something novel and unique, a work nevertheless must involve at least a modicum of creativity in order to receive copyright protection.

It is difficult to pinpoint exactly what is required in order to satisfy the creativity requirement. At one time, courts applied a "sweat of the brow" rule according to which the amount of effort put into a work determined whether it was creative or not. Facts and information could be protected by copyright if the researcher or compiler worked hard to investigate and gather them. That doctrine has been abolished, however. No matter how difficult a research project or fact compilation is, facts and information simply are not protected by copyright.

Today, creativity is assessed by neither a qualitative nor a quantitative analysis.

Unfortunately, there is no bright-line test for determining whether something is sufficiently creative to warrant copyright protection or not. It is possible, however, to identify certain kinds of things that are deemed to be too uncreative to receive copyright protection:

- Titles
- Names
- Short phrases
- *Scènes à faire*
- Jokes and gags
- Blank forms
- Fact gathering
- Alphabetization
- Consecutive numbering
- Page numbers
- Geometric shapes
- Familiar symbols
- Uncreative compilation methods.

This is not an exhaustive list.

SCÈNES À FAIRE

A *scène à faire* is a stock or standard literary device, typically in a play or other dramatic work. It is a scene or detail that is considered standard in works in a particular genre. Uses of gadgetry in a spy novel, or a male serenading a lady outside her window in a romance, are examples. *Scènes à faire* do not receive copyright protection.

In a similar vein, similarities between a scene in one work and a scene in another work do not infringe a copyright in the first work if they follow naturally from the situation. A couple seeking refuge in a church during a storm would be an example.

Stereotypical characters do not receive copyright protection, either. The description of a character as a drunken Irish policeman, for example, is not protected by copyright.

Details that are essential to the description of a particular kind of scene are also considered *scènes à faire.* It has been held, for example, that a movie about the South Bronx featuring drunks, prostitutes, vermin, and junk cars does not infringe the copyright in a previous movie featuring those same things. According to the court, any movie about the South Bronx would need to feature these things in order to be realistic.

Placing a list of variables at the beginning of the source code of a computer program is another example of a *scène à faire.* The textual content of the list might be protected by copyright, but the practice of listing variables at the beginning is so standard that no one can claim a copyright in this kind of arrangement.

Music

The rule of thumb for musical works is that both the melody and the lyrics of a song are protected by copyright if they are original. Use of either the music alone or the lyrics alone is just as capable of being infringement as use of the words and music together is. Other elements—the beat, rhythm, chord progression, and fills – usually are not protected by copyright.

Song titles and short musical (or lyrical) phrases are not protected by copyright. They may be trademarks, though, if they are used in connection with the marketing of goods or services. "Ziggy Stardust" and "Yellow Submarine" are examples of song titles which, although not protected by copyright, are protected trademarks. Taylor Swift and other popular recording artists have registered a number of their song titles and lyrical phrases as trademarks.

Originality

To receive copyright protection, a work must be original, meaning that an author must create the work independently, not by copying another work. Logically, this is simply an aspect of the creativity requirement. Courts, however, sometimes treat it as a separate requirement.

Originality is required whether the copied work is protected by copyright or not. Accordingly, neither a work that is created by copying a public domain work nor a work that is created by copying a copyright protected work receives copyright protection.

Because of the originality requirement, the creator of an authorized derivative work only acquires a copyright in the newly created aspects of the derivative work, not in the original work.

The creator of an unauthorized derivative work does not acquire a copyright in any aspect of the derivative work.

INDEPENDENT CREATION

When two or more authors create the same work without either working cooperatively or copying each other, then each is an author and each owns a copyright in the work. If, for example, two musicians write the same song without either of them being aware of the other, then neither of them is guilty of infringement, and each of them may sue others for infringement of the copyright. The two works must truly be created independently, though. If one author copied the other – even subconsciously—then the work that is a copy of the other would not meet the originality requirement and therefore would not receive copyright protection.

In those rare cases where two authors do independently create identical or very similar works without either one copying the other, they are not joint authors. They are each individual authors of the work, each with protectable copyrights.

Photographs and Drawings of Other Works

A person who photographs or draws another person's drawing or photograph generally does not have any protected copyright interest in the photograph or drawing so created. Because the taking of a photograph is a means of copying the subject of the photograph, photographing a drawing or other preexisting work infringes the copyright owner's exclusive right of reproduction of the work. Again, no copyright is acquired through infringement.

Drawing or photographing existing works would also infringe the copyright owner's exclusive right to make derivative works. A modified version of a copyrighted work would be a derivative work. Only the copyright owner has the right to make derivative works from her work. An infringer acquires no copyright in an unauthorized derivative work.

Photographing or drawing a copy of public domain material is not infringement. Therefore, such photographs and drawings may be protected by copyright. Owners of the copyrights in such photographs and drawings do not acquire rights in the underlying works, though. The underlying works remain in the public domain.

Although pushing a button on a camera is considered a creative act, courts have held that photographs of other works are not entitled to copyright protection when they involve only slavish copying. Slavishly photographing, scanning or digitizing a preexisting work will not result in the creation of a new copyrightable work if the copy is identical in visual appearance to the original, even if the work in question is in the public domain. An unretouched photograph of the Mona Lisa, for example, normally will not be protected by copyright.

Human creation

Copyright only protects works that are created by human beings. There is no copyright protection for materials that are created by natural forces, machines, or nonhuman animals.

Machine-generated output that is created without any human interaction is not protected by copyright. A human may use a machine to assist in the fixation of a work, and the work that is fixed in a medium of expression as a result may be protected by copyright, but if the machine itself actually creates the output, then it is not.

Exclusive rights

A copyright owner has the following exclusive rights:

- Reproduction
- Distribution
- Public display
- Public performance
- Making of derivative works.

The owner of a copyright in a sound recording has an exclusive right to digitally perform it, but not to publicly perform it by other means.

Exceptions

A person may copy, distribute, publicly display, publicly perform or create a derivative work based on another person's work without incurring copyright infringement liability in 4 situations:

- Public domain (i.e., copyright either never existed or has ceased to exist)
- Fair use
- License or assignment of rights
- Work made for hire.

Copyright defenses are not defenses against trademark infringement or other kinds of claims.

Co-authorship

As a general rule, if two or more people work together to create a work, then in the absence of an agreement otherwise, they own the copyright jointly, provided they each contribute copyrightable expression.

Whether a work is jointly owned, or whether an element of it is owned separately by the creator of that element, is a question of intent. When two or more people create a work with the intention that their respective contributions will be merged into inseparable or interdependent parts of a unitary whole, then they are joint owners of the resulting work. Otherwise, each one is an individual owner of his or her individual contribution to the work.

Owners of the copyright in a joint work are tenants in common. That is to say, they each own an undivided, fractional interest in the copyright. Each joint owner is free to exercise any of the rights of a copyright owner without needing to get the permission of the other joint owners. Each owner may license rights in the work to others. Each joint owner must account to the others, however, for any profits realized from either direct use or licensing of rights in the copyrighted work.

Works made for hire

The copyright in a work initially belongs to the author. Usually, the person who creates a work is the author. In the case of a work made for hire, however, an employer or a person who specially commissions the work is the author.

A work made for hire is one that is either:

- created by an employee in the course of the employment; or
- specially commissioned pursuant to an agreement in which the parties expressly agree, in writing, that the work will be considered a work made for hire.

Employee status is determined by the law of agency. Courts consider several factors to determine whether a person is an employee or an independent contractor. The right to supervise and control the hired person is probably the most significant factor, but no single factor is determinative.

A work created by an employee within the course and scope of employment is automatically a work made for hire even if there is no written agreement to that effect. A specially commissioned work, by contrast, is not a work made for hire unless the agreement between the contractor and the person commissioning the work expressly states that it is a work made for hire. The agreement must be signed and in writing.

Because the employer or person specially commissioning a work is treated as the author, the person who actually created a work made for hire will be guilty of infringement if s/he copies, publicly displays, distributes, publicly performs, or makes derivative works based on it without the employer's permission (or the permission of the person who specially commissioned the work).

A work is not a work made for hire unless it is either created during the course of the employment or created pursuant to the agreement commissioning it. If a writer/artist began creating the work before the employment began or before the agreement was made, then it cannot be a work made for hire. Thus, an author who creates a work and then enters into a contract with a publisher that specifies that the work is a work made for hire will continue to retain ownership of the copyright unless and until s/he assigns the copyright to the publisher.

In the absence of an employment relationship, only the following kinds of specially commissioned works can be made the subject of a work made for hire agreement:

- Contribution to a collective work
- Contribution to a motion picture or other audiovisual work
- Translation
- Supplementary work
- Compilation
- Instructional text

- Test (and/or answer material for a test)
- Atlas.

A supplementary work is one that is prepared as an adjunct to another work. Examples: preface, introduction, illustrations, revisions, commentary, foreword, afterword, annotations, musical arrangement, answer material for a test, bibliography, appendix, index, etc.

Only copyright protections are acquired by virtue of the fact that a work is a work made for hire. Trademark and other intellectual property rights are not.

Compilations

The selection and arrangement of things to include in a compilation can take some thought and creativity. For this reason, a compilation is considered a work of authorship on the part of the compiler. This means that the editor of a collection of stories, for example, may have a protected copyright interest in the selection and arrangement of the works in a collection – even if s/he did not author any of them.

Copyright protection for a compilation may exist even if the individual elements included in it are not protected by copyright. The selection of facts, and decisions about how to arrange and present them, may be protected by copyright even though the facts themselves are not. The selection and arrangement of a compilation of public domain works may be protected by copyright even though none of the works included in it is.

The copyright in the compilation and the copyright(s) in the individual works within it are separate things. An editor may own a copyright in the selection and arrangement aspects of a compilation of short stories, while an author of a story in the collection may own the copyright in the story.

The owner of the copyright in a compilation is presumed to possess the right to reproduce and distribute the works contributed to it only as part of that compilation or a revision of that compilation. Merely owning the copyright in a compilation does not give rise to a right to copy, publicly display or distribute—or to authorize others to copy, publicly display or distribute—an individual story or article that is included in the collection.

The owner of the compilation copyright has an exclusive right to make revisions to the compilation, such as by rearranging the order, adding new stories or information to it, or removing a story or fact from it. The author of a copyrighted work appearing in the compilation, however, has the exclusive right to make derivative works of his or her copyrighted work.

Copyright protection for a compilation does not confer copyright protection on portions of it that would not otherwise receive copyright protection. Owning the copyright in a data compilation does not confer ownership of the data, for example. If something would not be protected by copyright before it was compiled, then it will remain unprotected by copyright after the compilation. Only the manner in which the data is selected, arranged, presented or expressed in a compilation is protected by a copyright in the compilation.

Derivative works

A derivative work is one that contains elements of a preexisting work but with modifications. Examples: translations, dramatizations, fictionalizations, musical arrangements, screenplays, movie versions of novels, sound recordings of songs, lithographs based on paintings, drawings based on photographs, abridgements, condensations, adaptations, annotations, revisions, and updated websites. Incorporating programming code into another computer program results in the creation of a derivative work. A performance of a song is a derivative work of the song, as is a recording of the performance.

The copyright owner has an exclusive right to make derivative works from the work. No one else may do so without a license or permission from the copyright owner.

Copyrights cannot be acquired through infringement, so the maker of an unauthorized, infringing derivative work acquires no rights.

Ownership of a copyright in a derivative work only confers rights in the newly created aspects; it does not give the creator of the derivative work any rights in the original work.

Because anyone may freely use works that are in the public domain, derivative works based on public domain works are protected by copyright. The copyright in the derivative work does not confer ownership of a copyright in the original public domain work, though. Other people can make their own derivative works based on the same public domain work. The copyright in a derivative work only protects rights in material that is newly created for the derivative work.

Infringement

Infringement occurs when someone without a right or permission to do so exercises one of the exclusive rights of ownership of the copyright in a work (reproduction, distribution, public display, public performance, or the making of a derivative work).

Infringement may be direct or indirect. *Direct* infringement occurs when an act of infringement (copying, etc.) is committed by the person sought to be held liable for it. *Indirect* infringement occurs when one person commits the act of infringement and another person is held responsible for it.

There are 3 kinds of indirect infringement:

- Vicarious
- Contributory
- Inducement.

Direct infringement

A person who exercises one of the exclusive rights of a copyright owner without authority or permission may be liable for direct infringement of the copyright.

Reproduction

Reproduction means making a copy or copies of a work. The copy may be either identical or "substantially similar."

Copying may be proven with direct or circumstantial evidence. Direct evidence might include, for example, the testimony of an eyewitness who actually saw the copying occur.

Proof by circumstantial evidence requires a showing of **access + similarity**. A strong showing on one factor means that the showing on the other factor does not have to be as strong, but there must be at least some amount of evidence to support each. In rare cases, however, a court may find that the fact that two works are very strikingly similar serves as circumstantial evidence of access, as well.

The fame or wide public distribution of a work can provide circumstantial evidence of access, even if there is no direct evidence that the alleged infringer actually viewed or heard the work. In the case of an unpublished or obscure work, some direct evidence of an actual opportunity to see the work may be necessary (such as the fact that the author submitted the work to the person for possible use in a publication, for example).

The similarity may, but does not have to, involve copyrightable elements. If there has been a clear showing of access, then the existence of similar facts, ideas, public domain elements, etc. may help support an inference of copying. For example, even though a mis-typed word or other small error in a manuscript is not protectable by copyright, the same error (factual, typographical or grammatical) appearing in two works can provide strong circumstantial evidence of copying.

Public Display or Performance

Not all displays or performances of copyrighted material are infringement. Only public ones are. Anyone who lawfully acquires a copy of a copyrighted work may display or perform it privately.

Because public performance of a sound recording is not one of the exclusive rights of the owner of a copyright in a sound recording, publicly performing (playing) a sound recording does not infringe the copyright in the sound recording, although it might infringe the copyright in a musical or literary work that is performed in it. The owner of a copyright in a sound recording does have an exclusive right to publicly perform it by means of digital transmission (streaming), however.

DISTRIBUTION

Distribution means an actual transfer of a copy to another person.

Vicarious infringement

Vicarious infringement refers to the imputation of an infringing act to a person on whose behalf another person committed it. It may be imposed when a person has both:

(a) the right and the power to supervise a direct infringer; and
(b) a direct financial interest in the infringement.

Examples: employer and employee; principal and agent. Knowledge of the infringing activity is not necessary. A person with supervisory power over another person may be held vicariously liable for the person's infringing activity from which she benefits financially even if she had no idea that the person was engaging in infringing activity.

Contributory infringement

Contributory infringement means knowingly facilitating another person's act(s) of direct infringement. Three elements need to be established:

(1) Direct infringement
(2) Another person knew or should have known about it; and
(3) This other person materially contributed to the infringement.

Actual knowledge is not necessary. Contributory liability may be imposed if a reasonable person would infer, based on the facts known, that infringing activity is occurring.

A&M Records v. Napster[3] established, among other things, that if an online service provider knows or should know of actual ongoing infringement by a user of the service, and has the right and the ability to stop it, then failure to stop the infringing activity may suffice to establish contributory liability.

If a substantial non-infringing use for a facility or mechanism exists, then the mere fact that a person provided the facility or mechanism is not a "material contribution" to the infringement. In *Sony Corp. v. Universal City* Studios[4] the U.S. Supreme Court held that merely providing a mechanism that somebody could use or has used to engage in infringing activity is not enough to qualify as a material contribution to the infringement. There must be, in addition, some affirmative act of solicitation, inducement, encouragement, or assistance to another to use the facility or mechanism to infringe a copyright.

In both *Sony* and *Napster*, the copyright owners sued a provider of a means by which people were infringing copyrights. *Sony* involved a distributor of videocassette recording devices. *Napster* involved a provider of a peer-to-peer networking system.

Inducement

In *Metro-Goldwyn-Mayer Studios, Inc. v. Grokster, Ltd.*[5] the U.S. Supreme Court clarified that providing a mechanism that may be used to infringe copyrights, and inducing or encouraging its use for that purpose, may be enough to establish indirect liability for infringement. Failing to remove content upon learning that it infringes a copyright may qualify as "materially contributing" to the infringement if the service provider has the ability and power to remove the content upon learning of it. Inducing or encouraging the users of a peer-to-peer

---

[3] 239 F.3d 1004 (9th Cir. 2001).

[4] 464 U.S. 417 (1984).

[5] 545 U.S. 913 (2005).

networking system to use it to infringe copyrights also qualifies. Moreover, evidence that a person induced or encouraged infringing activity may also supply the "reason to know" that infringing activity would occur.

Innocent infringement

Innocent infringement generally does not absolve a person of liability for infringement. Good faith, ignorance or a lack of intent to infringe generally are not defenses to copyright infringement. There is one situation where innocent infringement may be a complete defense to infringement, though. If the person named in the copyright notice appearing on copies of the work is not the copyright owner, then the defendant may assert the defense in an infringement action by proving that he was misled by the notice and that he used the work in good faith based on a purported transfer or license from the person named in that notice. This defense, however, is available only if (a) the work was not registered in the name of the copyright owner before the infringement began, and (b) no document executed by the person named in the notice and showing the ownership of the copyright was recorded before the infringement began.

Although not a defense, proof that infringement was not done knowingly may reduce the amount of statutory damages that may be awarded.

Noncommercial use

The fact that no profit or commercial benefit was gained is not a defense to infringement. It may reduce the amount of damages, and in some situations, it may help support a fair use defense, but it is not a stand-alone defense.

Remedies

Both civil and criminal remedies are available for the enforcement of copyrights.

Injunctions

A court may issue injunctive relief against copyright infringement. This includes both preliminary and permanent injunctions.

Damages

ACTUAL DAMAGES

Actual damages are the out-of-pocket losses and loss of profits the copyright owner has experienced as a result of the infringement. A court may also require the defendant to pay the plaintiff the amount of the profit he has earned from the infringing use. There cannot be a double recovery, however. If included as an element of actual damages, lost profits cannot be awarded separately.

STATUTORY DAMAGES

In lieu of actual damages and profits, a court may instead award statutory damages in an amount specified by the Copyright Act. No proof of actual damage is necessary if a plaintiff qualifies and opts for an award of statutory damages.

The amount of statutory damages that may be awarded ranges from $750 to $30,000. If the infringement is willful, the amount may be increased to $150,000. The amount of statutory damages may be reduced to as little as $200, however, if the infringement was innocent, i.e., done without the infringer's notice or knowledge that he was infringing a copyright. Registration, if effected before the infringement begins, can forestall a claim of innocent infringement.

Willful infringement occurs when the defendant either (a) actually knew that his acts infringed a copyright; or (b) acted with deliberate blindness to, or reckless disregard for, the copyright holder's rights.

Only a single award of statutory damages may be made on account of infringing activity by the same defendant with respect to the same work, no matter how many distinct acts of infringement the defendant committed with respect to that work. A separate award of statutory damages may be made with respect to each work that is infringed.

Statutory damages may not be awarded against nonprofit educational institutions, libraries or public broadcasting entities that had reasonable grounds to believe that the challenged activity was fair use. A person who sues one of these kinds of entities for copyright infringement will need to prove actual damages or lost profits.

Statutory damages may be elected only if the work is registered either before the infringement begins or within three months after the first publication of the work. If the infringement began before the work was registered, and more than three months have gone by since the work was first published, then statutory damages will not be available.

Affixing a copyright notice substantially reduces the amount of statutory damages that may be recovered – potentially to as little as \$200—if the infringer did not have notice or knowledge of the copyright through other means.

Attorney fees and costs may be awarded. Timely registration can affect a claimant's eligibility for an award of attorney fees for infringement. Normally, attorney fees may be awarded to either party, on the basis of which party prevails. Attorney fees may be awarded to a copyright infringement claimant, however, only if, in addition to winning the case, the work was registered either before the infringement occurred or within three months after first publication.

Impoundment

A court may order the impoundment of infringing copies. The means by which copies are made (such as molds, plates, computers,

CD burners, etc.) may also be seized. At the conclusion of the proceeding, a court may order that infringing copies be either destroyed or turned over the plaintiff.

Criminal penalties

Willful copyright infringement is a crime. For a first offense, imprisonment for up to five years and a fine of up to $250,000 may be imposed. Imprisonment for up to ten years and a fine of up to $250,000 may be imposed for a second offense.

Fraudulent removal or use of a copyright notice is also a crime, as is the making of a false representation to the Copyright Office in connection with an application for registration. The DMCA makes circumventing copyright protection measures a crime, in some circumstances. It also makes dealing in copyright protection circumvention products unlawful.

Preemption

The 1976 Copyright Act expressly preempts state law.

A state law claim is preempted if both of the following conditions exist:

- The state law remedy vindicates a right that is equivalent to one of the exclusive rights of a copyright owner; and
- The material is of a kind the Copyright Act protects.

If the Copyright Act, by its terms, does not provide protection for a particular kind of material, then a state law claim is not preempted. Thus, the Copyright Act does not preempt state law remedies for the appropriation of information, ideas or personality.

A state law claim that is not the equivalent of one of the exclusive rights of copyright ownership is not preempted, either. For this reason, courts generally hold that state law claims for breach of contract of a voluntary copyright licensing agreement are not preempted. On the other hand, enforcement of a contract provision prohibiting acts that would constitute copyright infringement may be deemed preempted, since enforcing such a provision would be tantamount to enforcing the Copyright Act's prohibition against infringement.

State laws authorizing causes of action for conduct that federal copyright law declares to be fair use are preempted. People may enter into enforceable contractual waivers of federally protected rights, though. Therefore, even though a state cannot enact a law prohibiting reverse engineering, a provision in a software licensing contract that prohibits it may be enforceable.

Copyright Claims Board

In 2022, a new administrative tribunal within the U.S. Copyright Office began hearing cases. This new tribunal is designed to process the following types of cases:

- Copyright infringement
- Declaration of non-infringement
- Misrepresentation in a DMCA notification or counter-notification.

This new tribunal, called the Copyright Claims Board, can hear and decide claims in which the amount of the claim does not exceed $30,000. It does not have the authority to issue or enforce injunctions.

The same kinds of defenses can be raised as can be raised in a court action. Unlike a copyright infringement complaint filed in federal court, however, it is not necessary for the plaintiff to have received either a registration certificate or a denial of registration before filing a claim. Filing a registration application will suffice.

It is a voluntary process, i.e., a claimant may choose to file either in court or with the Copyright Claims Board and a defendant may opt out of having the matter decided by the Board.

The board has its own sets of rules of procedure and evidence. They are intended to be simpler and more streamlined than the Federal Rules of Civil Procedure and The Federal Rules of Evidence.

Standard defenses

General denial

Consent

Consent may be manifested in a licensing agreement or in other ways. The defense is lost to the extent the use exceeds the scope of the consent given.

Consent may be express or implied. Implied consent may arise from circumstances that would lead a reasonable person to believe the copyright owner has given permission for what would otherwise be an infringing use. A book containing what the cover describes as "easy-to-use forms" is an example where implied consent to copy for personal use has been given. Distributing copies of the forms to other people, however, would exceed the scope of an implied license to copy forms for one's own use.

First sale

The copyright owner's exclusive right to distribute a particular embodiment of a work generally is exhausted upon the first sale or transfer of title to the copy, provided the copy was lawfully made and acquired. The owner of a particular copy that has been lawfully made and acquired usually is entitled to sell, rent or otherwise dispose of its possession without needing permission from the copyright owner.

The first sale doctrine only applies to the right to distribute the lawfully owned copy. The copyright owner's other exclusive rights are not exhausted upon the first sale. Lawfully owning a copy does not confer the right to make additional copies, publicly perform, publicly display, or make derivative works based on the work.

The first sale doctrine only applies to transfers of ownership of a copy. It does not apply to rented or licensed properties. Most copies of software are licensed, not sold. In these situations, the buyer's rights are governed by the terms of the rental or licensing agreement rather, not the first sale doctrine.

Computer programs and sound recordings of musical works are exceptions to the first sale doctrine.

An object embodying a computer program may be rented, leased or loaned, however, if the object is a machine and cannot be copied during the ordinary operation or use of the machine.

Videogames (i.e., computer programs embodied in or used in conjunction with a limited purpose computer that is designed for playing video games) may be rented, leased or loaned. Computer video games, i.e., games that can be played on a general-purpose computer, do not fall into this category.

The first sale doctrine is not a defense to a digital transfer of a lawfully acquired digital copy of any kind of work. Digital transfers involve the making of a copy. The first sale doctrine only applies to the distribution right, not the reproduction right.

Statute of limitations

A copyright infringement action must be commenced within three years from the date of the last infringement. The statute of limitations does not bar an infringement action if the infringement began more than three years prior to the commencement of the lawsuit if the infringement was still going on at some time during the three-year period before the lawsuit is commenced. Damages (and/or profits) may be recovered only for the infringement occurring during the three-year period prior to the commencement of the lawsuit, however.

The statute of limitations for copyright crimes is five years.

Equitable estoppel

Estoppel is another equitable defense that may be available in some cases. Elements of the defense are:

(a) knowledge of a fact on the part of the claimant
(b) lack of knowledge of the fact by the defendant
(c) intent to induce the defendant to act upon the claimant's representation or conduct, or conduct that made it reasonable to believe he had that intent
(d) Reliance on claimant's representation or conduct to the defendant's detriment.

Abandonment

Abandonment is a defense that may be asserted when a copyright claimant evidences an intention to surrender rights to the copyright in the work, and to allow the public to copy it. Examples include: voluntary dedication to the public domain, such as by placing a notice on a copy of a work that it may be freely copied; knowing failure to take action against widespread infringement; or intentionally destroying the only copy of a videotape of a live broadcast.

Prior to 1989, distributing a copy of a work without a copyright notice affixed to it was treated as abandonment. Since the notice is not required for works published after March, 1989, failing to affix it to a work published after 1989 no longer operates as abandonment of the copyright.

Copyright misuse

A court may deny relief to a copyright owner who has engaged in misconduct in connection with obtaining or enforcing the copyright. There are two kinds:

- antitrust violation involving a copyright; or
- use of copyright or copyright law in a way that violates the policy of copyright law.

Examples:

- Making false or misleading statements to the Copyright Office
- Unfair dealing with an alleged infringer
- A provision in a licensing agreement that prohibits the licensee from creating its own original creative works.

The defense does not require proof of any particular injury to the defendant. The relevant consideration is the adverse impact on the public interest.

Copyright misuse does not invalidate the owner's copyright. It merely precludes its enforcement by a particular person during the period of the person's misuse. The defense may not be asserted against a person who has purged himself of the misuse.

First Amendment

The First Amendment is a potential defense to copyright infringement in cases where the material in question is a matter of public interest. Footage of the assassination of John F. Kennedy is an example. The scope of the defense is limited, however. Only that amount of copying that is needed to convey the idea is permitted. Unnecessary copying is not protected by the First Amendment. Much fair use jurisprudence is grounded in or at least greatly influenced by First Amendment values.

The public domain

When none of the exclusive rights of the kind that copyright law protects exist, a work is said to be in the public domain. No one owns a copyright in material that is in the public domain.

Material may be in the public domain either because it is a kind of subject matter that copyright law does not protect or because something has happened to cause it to lose its protection. Moreover, it is possible for some elements of a work to be in the public domain while others are not.

The fact that a work is in the public domain is not a defense to trademark, defamation, misappropriation of information, invasion of privacy, or other non-copyright claims.

Dedication to the public domain

The owner of the copyright in a work may voluntarily dedicate it to the public domain. This can be accomplished by including a statement with the work declaring that it is in (or is dedicated to) the public domain. The decision to release a work into the public domain is irrevocable.

Making a work available to the public for free is not the same thing as dedicating it to the public domain.

Only the copyright owner has the power to dedicate a work to the public domain.

Duration of copyrights

The current rule in the United States is that a copyright in a newly created work lasts for the life of the author plus 70 years. For coauthored works, the copyright lasts for the life of the last surviving author plus 70 years.

The rule is subject to three important exceptions:

- works made for hire
- anonymous or pseudonymous works
- certain older works.

The duration of a copyright is governed by the law of the country in which it came into existence. The United States and many other countries have entered into treaties for the protection and enforcement of foreign copyrights, as well as to achieve greater uniformity in the copyright laws of different countries. There are still variations among countries with respect to the duration of a copyright, however.

Works made for hire

The term of a copyright in a work made for hire in the United States is the earlier of:

- 95 years after publication; or
- 120 years after the work was first fixed in a tangible medium.

The term may be different for older works (See below).

Anonymous and pseudonymous works

The duration of a U.S. copyright in a newly created work by an anonymous or pseudonymous author is the same as that for a work made for hire, unless the author is identified before the term of the copyright expires. If that happens, then the copyright lasts for the life of the author plus seventy years. The term may be different for older woks, as discussed below.

Works published or registered before January 1, 1978

Today, copyright is exclusively a matter of federal law. Prior to 1978, however, federal copyright protection existed only for works that either had been published with a copyright notice or registered with the U.S. Copyright Office. Until a work was published or registered, an author had only common law copyright rights under state law.

The 1976 Copyright Act, which became effective January 1, 1978, preempted the field of copyright, extending federal copyright protection to authors immediately upon the fixation of a work in a tangible medium. With the 1976 Act, publication or registration was no longer a prerequisite for federal copyright protection.

Before 1978, copyrights were renewable. A copyright that was still in its original term could be renewed for a second term. Effective January 1, 1978, the 1976 Act replaced the system of renewable fixed-term copyrights with a single term. Initially, the Act set the new single term at the life of the author plus 50 years. The 50-year period was later extended to 70 years.

The term of a copyright in a work that was published or registered before January 1, 1978, however, is not measured this way. The duration or a copyright in a work that was published or registered before January 1, 1978 must be determined by applying the law that was in effect at the time the work was published or registered.

"Publication"

Publication, for purposes of the public domain rules, means either:

(a) an authorized distribution of copies to the public; or
(b) an authorized offer to distribute copies to the public.

Before January 1, 1978, publishing a sound recording of a musical or literary work only had the effect of publishing the sound recording. It did not have the effect of publishing the musical composition or literary work performed on it. Unless it was published as sheet music or in some other way, a musical work remained "unpublished" for copyright purposes despite the release of multiple copies of recordings of performances of the song. For this reason, it was a common practice for publishers and record companies to register musical works as unpublished works in order to secure the benefits of federal registration. Beginning with musical works first published after 1977, distributing copies of a sound recording of a performance of a musical composition is a publication of both the sound recording and the musical and/or literary work performed in it.

Sound recordings made before February 15, 1972

Copyright protection for sound recordings did not begin in the United States until February 15, 1972. Until 2018, sound recordings made in the United States before February 15, 1972 were not protected by federal copyright law, although the musical or literary works in them might be. The Classics Protection and Access Act,[6] enacted in October, 2018, provides federal copyright protection for sound recordings made before February 15, 1972. Under this Act, sound recordings published before 1923 will enter the public domain on January 1, 2022. Sound recordings first published between 1923 and 1946 are protected for 100 years. Those first published between 1947 and 1956 are protected for 110 years. Sound recordings first published between 1957 and February 15, 1972 are protected until February 15, 2067. Sound recordings made but not published before February 15, 1972 enter the public domain on February 16, 2067, even if they become published before then. These rules preempt any contrary state laws.

Original and renewal terms

The first U.S. copyright law, the Copyright Act of 1790, provided for a term of fourteen years, renewable for another fourteen years. In 1831, Congress extended the original term to twenty-eight years. The Copyright Act of 1909 extended the renewal term to twenty-eight years, as well. Copyright terms were measured from the date of first publication or registration, whichever occurred earlier. If properly renewed, a copyright could have a duration of up to fifty-six years from the earlier of the date of publication or the date of registration.

A copyright had to be renewed during the last year of the original term. Otherwise, it lapsed and the work entered the public domain. If an original registration had not been filed yet, that had to be done before a renewal could be registered.

---

[6] Pub. L. 115–264 (codified at 17 U.S.C. §§ 301(c) and 1401).

A series of Congressional enactments beginning in 1962 and continuing into the 1970s extended the lengths of renewal terms of copyrights that were in their renewal terms at the time of the enactment. These enactments affected copyrights that had been secured (registered or first published) between September 19, 1906 and December 31, 1918, to the extent they had been timely and properly renewed prior to the enactment in question. The intent was to prevent copyrights from expiring before a new copyright law (ultimately, the Copyright Act of 1976) could be enacted. If a copyright had lapsed due to a failure to timely renew it during the last year of the original term, then it was lost. These enactments did not revive lapsed copyrights.

For those copyrights that were still in existence on January 1, 1978, the Copyright Act of 1976 increased the renewal term from twenty-eight to forty-seven years. This meant that for any copyright that was still in existence on January 1, 1978, the total possible duration of copyright (original + renewal terms) became seventy-five years. The extension applied to any copyrights that were either in their original term on January 1, 1978, or in their renewal term at any time between December 31, 1976 and December 31, 1977, inclusive. The extension also applied to copyrights that were in the last year of their original term between December 31, 1976 and December 31, 1977, inclusive, provided a timely renewal application had been filed.

The Sonny Bono Copyright Term Extension Act of 1998[7] added twenty more years to the renewal term, extending the renewal term to sixty-seven years. This extension applied to all renewable copyrights that were still in existence on October 27, 1998.

Tying copyright terms to calendar years

The 1976 Copyright Act extended the term of each copyright that was still in existence on January 1, 1978 to the end of the calendar year in which it would otherwise expire. This also applies to all copyrights that come into existence on or after January 1, 1978.

---

[7] Pub. L. 105–298, 112 Stat. 2827

Automatic renewal of certain pre-1978 works

1992 amendments to the Copyright Act made renewal automatic for those works that were still in their original term on June 26, 1992. This meant that for works first published or registered between January 1, 1964, and December 31, 1977, inclusive, it was no longer necessary to apply for renewal; it happened automatically.

The elimination of the renewal requirement does not apply retroactively. The transition to a single-term system did not restore the copyrights in works that had already entered the public domain due to failure to renew the copyright before the expiration of the original term.

Although renewal registration is no longer required beginning June 26, 1992, the Act permits any renewable copyright that was still in its original term as of June 26, 1992 to be registered anytime during the renewal period. For works that were in their original terms on June 26, 1992, failure to file a renewal registration prior to the expiration of the original term no longer results in forfeiture of copyright protection, though.

Filing an application to renew a registration during the last year of the original term may not be necessary, but it has some benefits. A renewal registration that is filed during the last year of the original term gives rise to a presumption of validity of the copyright and of the facts set forth in the registration. A renewal registration that is filed during the renewal term does not have that effect.

Ownership of the renewal right

Even if someone else owns the copyright, the author generally owns the renewal right. When the author dies, the renewal right descends to:

- the widow, widower, or children of the author
- if no widow, widower or children, then the author's executor
- if no will, widow, widower or children, then the author's next of kin.

These rules are subject to some exceptions.

Posthumous Works

A *posthumous work* is one that was not published during the author's lifetime, i.e., one that has been published, if at all, only after the author died. If the author of a posthumous work did not assign the copyright or exploit any rights in the work during his lifetime, then the owner of the copyright owns the renewal right, too. The owner of the copyright upon an author's death is not necessarily the author's widow, widower, children, executor or next of kin. Since a copyright is personal property, a copyright owner's will or a state's intestacy laws may provide for a different disposition.

Works Made for Hire

The employer (or person who commissioned the work made for hire) owns the right to renew it. The actual creator of the work has no renewal rights, nor do that person's heirs.

Transfers of the renewal right

Copyright law reserves to the author the right to renew the copyright even if she transfers ownership of the copyright to someone else. In addition, the renewal copyright may be conveyed separately from the original copyright. Thus, the author may transfer ownership of the original copyright to one person while transferring the right of ownership of the copyright during the renewal term to someone else.

An author's transfer of the original term of a copyright is valid whether the author survives to the beginning of the renewal term or not. A transfer of a renewal copyright that is effected during the original term will not be valid, however, unless the author survives until the commencement of the renewal term. If the author dies during the original term, then the renewal right descends to his heirs, and the author's purported transfer of it to someone else is invalid.

A derivative work legitimately created by an assignee or licensee during the original term is subject to the renewal right. If the statutory heirs exercise the renewal right, then the maker of the derivative work will be liable for infringement if he continues to publicly distribute, perform, display or reproduce it after the copyright is renewed. If the original term expires during a time period when copyright renewal is automatic, then the maker of such a derivative work who continues to use it after the end of the original term will not be liable for infringement unless the statutory heirs (or their representative) actually file an application for renewal. (An application for renewal that is filed notwithstanding the fact that renewal is, by law, automatic is called a *permissive renewal.*) In no event, however, may new derivative works be made during the renewal period without the permission of the owner of the renewal term copyright.

Copyright notice

Copies of works published before 1978 needed to display a copyright notice. Failure to display a copyright notice on a published work would result in loss of copyright protection. Unless a work entered the public domain earlier for some other reason, the date of the first publication without a copyright notice was the date of entry into the public domain. Defects in the content or placement of a notice could also result in loss of copyright protection.

The copyright notice continued to be required for works first published after 1977 and before March 1, 1989. The requirements for an acceptable notice were similar to those for pre-1978 works, but not exactly the same.

Federal regulations changed from time to time during this period. The regulations that were in force on the date a work was published without a copyright notice control the determination of the adequacy of a copyright notice and the effect of defects in the notice.

As with pre-1978 works, the publication of a literary, musical or dramatic work on a phonorecord without a copyright notice could cause loss of copyright protection in the sound recording but not loss of copyright in the literary, musical or dramatic work embodied in it (unless, of course, lyrics and/or sheet music was also published.)

Omission of a proper copyright notice did not cause a work published during this period to enter the public domain in any of the following circumstances:

- It was omitted from only a small number of copies;
- It was removed without the copyright owner's authorization;
- The publisher had breached an express written agreement to place the notice on copies of the publication; or
- The copyright owner corrected the problem within five years of discovering it.

Some kinds of errors, although not causing a work to enter the public domain, could have other adverse consequences. Publication of a copyright notice erroneously naming the wrong person as the copyright owner could be corrected by registering the work in the name of the actual owner or recording a document executed by the person named in the notice that shows the correct ownership. If this was not done, however, then an innocent infringer who was misled by the notice and obtained an assignment or license from the person named in the notice would have a complete defense against a claim of infringement.

If the only error is that the date indicated in a copyright notice that has been placed on a published work is earlier than the actual date of publication, then the work does not enter the public domain as a result of the error. Instead, the term of copyright is deemed to begin in the copyright year indicated in the notice, not the year of actual publication. A copyright notice that indicates a year later than the actual date of publication does not have this effect. In this situation, the actual year of publication marks the beginning of the copyright term.

A copyright notice containing a date that is more than a year after the actual date of publication is treated as a complete omission of a copyright notice. Subject to the exceptions noted above, such an omission would cause the work to enter the public domain.

Elimination of the notice requirement

The Berne Convention for the Protection of Literary and Artistic Works of 1886 provides that copyright enforceability should not be made to depend on compliance with formalities. The United States became a signatory to the Berne Convention in 1988. The Berne Convention Implementation Act became effective on March 1, 1989. It provides that for works first published in the United States on or after March 1, 1989, the copyright notice is optional. Publication without the copyright notice does not cause such works to lose copyright protection. Elimination of the notice requirement is not retroactive, however. With the exception of certain foreign works that may be restored from the public domain, the entry of a work into the public domain is irreversible.

Manufacturing requirement

Books, periodicals, lithographs and photoengravings published before July 1, 1986 were required to be manufactured in the United States in order to receive federal copyright protection. The rule was subject to a variety of exceptions. This requirement has been abolished.

Restoration of copyrights in foreign works

To comply with international treaties, Congress has provided for the restoration of copyrights in certain foreign works. To be eligible for restoration, each of the following conditions must exist:

(a) At least one author was a citizen or domiciliary of a foreign country that is a signatory to the Agreement on Trade-Related Aspects of Intellectual Property Rights (TRIPS Agreement), the

Berne Convention, the World Intellectual Property Organization (WIPO) Copyright Treaty or Performances and Phonograms Treaty, or the subject of a proclamation under 17 U.S.C. § 104A(g); or the work must have been first published in such a country and not published in the United States within thirty days thereafter;

(b) The work is still protected by copyright in its nation of origin;

(c) It is in the public domain in the United States only because of one the following: (i) failure to satisfy a formality (such as registration, renewal, copyright notice, manufacturing requirement); (ii) origination in a country that did not have copyright relations with the United States; or (iii) it is a sound recording that was fixed in a tangible medium before February 15, 1972.

A "foreign work" is any work that does not fit into any of the following categories:

- first published in the United States
- first published simultaneously in the United States and in a foreign country that has an applicable treaty with the United States, and whose law provides for a copyright term that is at least as long as what U.S. law provides
- first published simultaneously in the United States and a foreign country that does not have an applicable treaty with the United States
- first published in a foreign country that does not have an applicable treaty with the United States, but all authors are nationals, domiciliaries, or habitual residents of the United States (or in the case of a motion picture, all authors are legal entities headquartered in the United States)
- unpublished work, and all authors are nationals, domiciliaries, or habitual residents of the United States (or in the case of a motion picture, all authors are legal entities headquartered in the United States)
- pictorial, graphic, or sculptural work that is incorporated into a building or structure that is located in the United States.

Copyright restoration went into effect on January 1, 1996, for foreign works from countries that were, on that date, members of the World Trade Organization (WTO); adherents to the Berne Convention, the WIPO Copyright Treaty or the WIPO Performances and Phonograms Treaty; or the subject of a proclamation under 17 U.S.C. § 104A(g). Copyright restoration for works from other countries went into effect on the earliest adherence date of the country to one of these treaties or the proclamation date, as applicable.

The duration of a restored copyright is the same as it would have been if it had never entered the public domain.

Pursuant to the Uruguay Round Agreements Act[299] (URAA), copyrights in the described foreign works are automatically restored. No action is required on the part of a copyright owner. An owner of a restored copyright may choose to register the copyright, however.

A person who relied on the public domain status of a foreign work before its copyright was restored is called a *reliance party*. A reliance party is liable for infringement only if (a) the foreign copyright owner filed notice with the U.S. Copyright Office within twenty-four months after the enactment of the URAA (i.e., no later than December 8, 1996), or (b) the foreign copyright owner served notice of intent to enforce the copyright directly on the person. In that event, the person so served may continue to exploit the work for twelve months after receiving the notice.

A reliance party may continue to exploit derivative works that are based on a restored copyright, but must pay reasonable compensation for them.

To be eligible for renewal registration, a foreign work that was first published or registered before 1978 must either have been published with the statutory or UCC notice or made the subject of an ad interim registration, on one hand, or registered as an unpublished work, on the other. In addition, it must have met all statutory requirements to maintain copyright through the full original term and into the renewal term. A work that failed to secure copyright in the United States at the time of first publication, or lost it at any time during the original or renewal terms, is not eligible for renewal registration even if copyright was restored in the United States under the URAA.

Works created but not published or registered before 1978

For works created but not published or registered before January 1, 1978, copyright protection generally lasts for the life of the author (or in the case of joint works, the life of the last surviving author) plus 70 years, or December 31, 2002, whichever is later. If an unpublished work created before January 1, 1978 is published before December 31, 2002, then the term is extended to the life of the author plus 70 years or December 31, 2047, whichever is later.

The copyright in an unpublished work made for hire, or an anonymous or pseudonymous work, that was created before January 1, 1978, lasts for 120 years from the year of creation or ninety-five years from the date of first publication, whichever expires first, but in no event earlier than December 31, 2002. If it is published before December 31, 2002, then the term is extended to December 31, 2047.

If the author of an anonymous or pseudonymous work is identified, and a statement of identity in proper form is timely and properly filed with the Copyright Office before the end of the term of the copyright, then the term of the copyright is governed by the same rules that apply to works created by an identified author.

Presumption of death

There is a rebuttable presumption that at the earlier of 95 years after first publication or 120 years after fixation in tangible form, the author has been dead for 70 years. To avoid premature loss of copyright protection, the copyright owner (or the author's estate) must file a statement of living status, or a date of death, with the Copyright Office. This must be done before the earlier of 95 years after publication or 120 years after fixation in tangible form. If it is not done within that time period, then the copyright expires.

Fair use

Granting a work's creator an exclusive right to exploit it generally promotes the public welfare by ensuring that artists and inventors will have an incentive to create new things. There may be circumstances, though, in which Congress or the courts determine that a greater public benefit is served by allowing people to use copyright-protected material without having to obtain the owner's permission. In such cases, the infringing use is declared to be "fair use." A person cannot be prosecuted or held liable for damages for making "fair use" of a copyrighted work.

Fair use is an affirmative defense. A person who asserts this defense is essentially acknowledging that infringement may have occurred, but claims the infringement is justified. A person who invokes the fair use defense has the burden of proving it.

Contrary to popular belief, there is no rule to the effect that a specified number of words in a text or a specified number of notes in a song is fair use. Aside from some narrowly defined safe harbors that Congress has created, the content of the fair use doctrine is developed by the courts on a case-by-case basis. They apply four broadly worded factors that frequently conflict, with no guidance from Congress about what to do when one factor supports a finding of fair use while another factor does not.

The four-factor test

A use of a copyrighted work may qualify as fair use if, after considering all relevant factors, a court determines that an important public policy outweighs the copyright owner's interest in controlling and receiving compensation for his or her work. 17 U.S.C. § 107 provides:

> [T]he fair use of a copyrighted work, including such use by reproduction in copies or phonorecords or by any

> other means … for purposes such as criticism, comment, news reporting, teaching (including multiple copies for classroom use), scholarship, or research, is not an infringement of copyright....

The statute directs courts to consider four factors:

- Purpose and character of the use
- Nature of work
- Amount and substantiality of the portion used
- Effect of the use on the market for the work.

The enumerated uses (criticism, commentary, teaching, etc.) are not safe harbors. These kinds of uses are likely to be fair use, but they are not always. A court must evaluate the four factors to make a determination.

Courts are not limited to the four factors. They may consider any other relevant factors.

Purpose and Character of the Use

Uses for the purposes listed in Section 107 (criticism, commentary, teaching, etc.) are likely to result in a finding that the first factor weighs in favor of a fair use determination. Of course, the other three factors will still need to be considered.

Although it is not dispositive of the issue, commercial use is usually less likely to be considered fair use than noncommercial or nonprofit use is. Making copies of a work solely for the purpose of selling or to spare someone the expense of buying a retail copy is highly unlikely to be deemed fair use. The fact that only noncommercial use of a work is made does not assure that it is fair use, however. Courts will consider the other three factors, too.

Parody is usually fair use even if it is published for a commercial purpose. This is because it is essentially criticism or commentary about the original work itself. It usually has no significant effect on the market for the original work because it does not compete in the market for the work itself. Copying more than what is needed is not fair use, but how much is needed for an effective parody is difficult to say.

Satire is not as likely to qualify as fair use. A parody targets and mimics the original work to criticize or comment on the work itself. A satire may mimic the original work, too, but not for the purpose of criticizing or commenting on it. A satire may criticize or comment on something else, such as social mores or political institutions, but the purpose of a satire is not to criticize or comment on the work itself. There is a greater need to copy a work, or portions of it to criticize or comment on it than there is to copy a work in connection with criticizing or commenting on something else.

A **transformative** use is any use that alters the purpose, meaning or function of a work, or a portion of it. It is any use that makes the work serve a purpose, express a meaning, or function in a way that is different from the purpose, meaning or function of the original work.

The U.S. Supreme Court has held that the more transformative a new work is, the more likely it is to be fair use. In *Campbell v. Acuff-Rose* Music[8] the Court reviewed rap group 2 Live Crew's unauthorized reproduction of the opening musical intro and first line of the Roy Orbison song, "Oh, Pretty Woman" for use in a song they called, "Pretty Woman." The U.S. Supreme Court held that 2 Live Crew's use of the song without permission was fair use because the group had transformed the song in such a way that the copied portions communicated a different meaning than the original song did. This, the Court ruled, outweighed the other factors, including the fact that 2 Live Crew had copied the "heart" of the song and that the group's commercial exploitation of Orbison's recording negatively impacted the market for the original.

Despite the Supreme Court's ruling, not every transformative use is fair use. For example, in *Warner Bros. Entertainment, Inc. v. RDR Books*[309] a court held that an encyclopedia of terms and lexicons used in Harry

---

[8] 510 U.S. 569 (1994).

Potter novels is not fair use. Although transformative, the court held it was nevertheless an infringing derivative work. A number of other cases have concluded that the unauthorized use of elements of a preexisting copyrighted work to make a derivative work is not fair use even though the copied elements were used for an entirely different purpose. For example, although parody is generally held to be fair use, courts have held that satire is not. Yet satire, by definition, makes use of elements of a work for a purpose that is entirely different from the original. The purpose of a satire may be to make a reader laugh or to criticize a social or political institution, person or event, but it rarely, if ever, conveys the same meaning or is used for the same purpose as the original. Nevertheless, some courts decline to hold that satire is fair use, at least if the amount and substantiality of the portions copied are significant.

Copying books to a digital format for use in a searchable database can be sufficiently transformative to be fair use. A court has also held that the fair use doctrine means Google Books may make unauthorized copies of over 30,000,000 books, without paying royalties to the authors, so that the company can create a searchable book index that reproduces and displays portions of the books to users in response to their search requests.

Downloading a copyrighted image, converting it into a thumbnail, and then displaying the thumbnail would infringe a copyright owner's exclusive rights to reproduce, display and make derivative works of the image. On the other hand, merely providing a link to a website where the image is being displayed with the copyright owner's permission would not infringe any of the copyright owner's exclusive rights. No copy is made; providing a link does not "display" anything; and no modification is made to the content of the image.

Inline linking is the placement of a special type of link in the web page coding that enables a viewer of the page to see a file that is hosted on a separate web page without leaving the original web page. In *Perfect 10, Inc. v. Google*,[9] the Ninth Circuit Court of Appeals ruled that

[9] 416 F. Supp. 2d 828 (C.D. Cal. 2006), *aff'd in part and rev'd in part*, 508 F.3d 1146 (9th Cir. 2007); *see also* Kelly v. Arriba Soft, 280 F.3d 934 (9th Cir. 2002).

providing a hypertext link, whether simple or inline, does not infringe reproduction or display rights. The image a user sees upon clicking a link is displayed as a result of the interaction between the user's system and the server on which the image is stored. The owner of the website providing the link does not "display" the copyrighted material itself.

Causing linked-to content to appear as thumbnails, however, does infringe the copyright owner's exclusive right to make derivative works.[10] In *Perfect 10 v. Amazon, Inc.*,[11] the Ninth Circuit Court of Appeals held that making thumbnails solely for inclusion in a searchable index is infringement but it is fair use. The court applied the four-factor test to determine that the public benefit of having a convenient Internet search engine outweighs the negative impact on the market for thumbnail versions of the copyrighted images. Because every application of the four-factor test is case-specific, it cannot be inferred from these cases that everyone may use inline linking to display thumbnail images of other people's images. To the contrary, it seems likely that if Google had not limited its use of the inline-thumbnail technology to an Internet search engine, it may have been held liable for copyright infringement.

Framing is the process of causing one website to be displayed in a frame on a screen simultaneously with that of another website. It raises a number of legal issues. If it is likely to create consumer confusion about the origin, sponsorship or endorsement of a product or service, it might constitute trademark infringement. The FTC might consider it a deceptive trade practice. In some cases, it might constitute misappropriation of information or unfair competition, if the conditions for those causes of action exist. Although an argument may be made that it does not infringe a copyright owner's reproduction or display rights, at least one court has held that causing copyrighted content to be displayed within a frame amounts to a modification of the original work, and if unauthorized, it infringes the copyright owner's exclusive right to create derivative works.[12]

---

[10] Perfect 10, Inc. v. Amazon.com, Inc., 508 F.3d 1146 (9th Cir. 2007).

[11] 487 F.3d 701, 719 (9th Cir. 2007)

[12] Futuredontics Inc. v. Applied Anagramic Inc., 1997 46 USPQ 2d 2005 (C.D. Cal.

Whether a particular kind of link amounts to direct infringement or not, it is clear that knowingly linking to a site that contains infringing content, or to a site that facilitates infringing activity, creates a risk of vicarious or contributory liability for the infringement that is occurring there.

THE NATURE OF THE WORK

Use of academic, scholarly, and other factual or practical works is more likely to be fair use than the use of fiction and other kinds of creative works is, but not all infringement of nonfiction works is automatically permitted as fair use. Unauthorized copying and distribution of such a substantial amount that the market for the work is adversely impacted is not likely to be considered fair use even if the work is nonfiction.

In general, it may be said that the less creativity or originality there is in the original work, the more likely that use of it is fair use.

When a copy of a work is difficult or impossible to obtain, unauthorized use of it is more likely to be fair use than would otherwise be the case. Of course, this will not be true if an organization is licensed to provide copies at a reasonable cost. Moreover, the fact that a copy of a work is difficult or impossible to obtain does not necessarily mean that every kind of use of it is automatically fair use. The four factors need to be evaluated to make that determination.

Because the right of first publication is valuable to authors, copying a published work is more likely to be deemed fair use than copying an unpublished work is.

AMOUNT AND SUBSTANTIALITY OF COPYING

Copying an entire work may qualify as fair use in some cases. Usually, though, copying an entire work is not likely to be fair use. Copying only a single word or note, by contrast, is not even

1997).

infringement at all. Stretched between these two extremes is a spectrum along which some amounts of copying are determined to be fair use and some are not. There are no hard-and-fast rules in this twilight zone, but a couple of general principles may be gleaned from the cases.

First, courts do not apply a numerical test. There is no legal rule that copying up to twenty words of text or four bars of music, or any other specified portion, is automatically fair use. Courts consider the importance of the portion(s) copied, not just the amount. Copying the portion of a work that gives it its popular appeal and commercial success— "the heart of the work"—is not as likely to be fair use as copying other elements of a work is. This is true even if the heart of the work comprises only one page in a four-hundred-page novel, or only a few bars of a song.

Courts also examine the purpose to which an infringer puts the copied portions of the work. A court is likely to hold that the copying is fair use if only the bare minimum needed for a core "fair use" purpose (criticism, commentary, etc.) is copied. The more the use relates to one of these purposes, the larger the amount of copying courts tend to tolerate, even if the copying involves substantial portions of the work. Conversely, copying more than what is needed for a core "fair use" purpose is not as likely to be considered fair use.

Effect on the Market for the Work

The effect of the use on the market for the original work is frequently, but not always, the deciding factor in fair use cases. A use is more likely to be deemed fair use if it does not compete against the copyrighted work in the same market. Conversely, a use is less likely to be deemed fair use if it competes in the same market with the original work. This is a principal reason that parodies are usually found to be fair use. A parody usually does not compete in the same market with the original work. Fans of the original work are not likely to be in the market for works that make fun of it.

The "amount and substantiality" factor often helps support a finding of the likely impact on the market for the original work. The smaller the amount of the original work that is copied, and the less substantial the parts copied are, the less likely the copying is to have an adverse effect on the market for the original work.

Both the actual effect of the defendant's conduct on current markets for the work and the projected effect on the market if the conduct were to become widely engaged in by others are considered.

If a use is for commercial gain, then the likelihood of a harmful effect on the market(s) for the author's work is presumed. If the use is for a noncommercial purpose, then the likelihood of a harmful impact on the market(s) for the author's work is not presumed; it must be proven. The presumption that a commercial use adversely affects the market for the original work is rebuttable. The best way to rebut it is to show that the work competes in a different market, so that sales of the new work do not detract from sales of the original work.

A finding that an infringing activity adversely affects the market for the original work may prevent a finding of fair use even if the infringer did not profit from the use. For example, making digital downloads available for free on the Internet harms the copyright holders' market for their works, and therefore is not fair use even though no profit is made from the activity.

Because the practice significantly reduces the market for the original work, using the Internet to exchange copies of copyrighted works with other users is not fair use. For the same reason, providing a service that facilitates such exchanges is not fair use.

Photocopying by a for-profit business usually is not fair use, even if the materials are only distributed internally. Similarly, systematic copying and distribution of journal articles to a business's employees is not often fair use.

If there is a ready means to pay for the use of a work and the user is a for-profit venture, using the work without paying for it is not likely to be fair use.

Statutory exemptions

Congress has declared certain kinds of uses to be fair use. When they apply, these exemptions from copyright infringement liability neither require nor permit consideration of the four factors.

The Copyright Act, as amended, is the source of some important statutory exemptions, such as ephemeral copies, transitory communications in which an online service provider acts only as a data conduit, system caching, Internet Service Providers (ISPs) providing users with a connection to the Internet, recipients of authorized broadcasts and transmissions, certain secondary transmissions, parental controls on motion pictures, computer operations such as decompilation, reverse engineering a computer program, non-simultaneous secondary transmissions by cable systems.

A photograph may be taken of a copyrighted work, such as a drawing or painting, that has been incorporated into a useful article, and the photograph may be used in news reports, commentary, and advertising related to the distribution or display of the useful article.

Under specified conditions, when a public or nonprofit institution of higher education is a service provider (e.g., provides access to the Internet, or maintains an informational or commercial website), it is exempt from liability for damages for the infringing activities of an employee on the basis that it transmitted, routed, or provided connections for, or engaged in system caching with respect to, infringing material transmitted at the employee's direction. This exemption only protects the institution from an award of damages. A court may still issue injunctive relief against the institution if infringing activity is found to have occurred.

An accredited nonprofit educational institution or a governmental body may display or perform copyrighted works in web-based instructional programs, provided the detailed conditions set out in the statute are satisfied.

Nondramatic musical works may be performed in classroom educational activities. This can include Internet transmissions, but only if relevant to the instructional content, and only if the transmission is made by or under the supervision of a teacher as part of a class session offered by a public school or an accredited nonprofit educational institution. This exemption does not apply to works that are specifically made or marketed for classroom instructional purposes, or to copies of works that were not lawfully obtained. A webcaster invoking this exception must employ technological measures to prevent recipients of the transmission from retaining the work for longer than the class session, and to prevent unauthorized further dissemination of the work. Also, the webcaster must not do anything that interferes with technological measures used by copyright owners to prevent such retention or unauthorized further dissemination.

Performance of a copyrighted musical work or nondramatic literary work, or of a dramatico-musical work of a religious nature, or display of a work, in the course of religious services at a place of worship is fair use. This exemption only covers performances at the place of worship. It does not apply to broadcasts or transmissions of religious services over the Internet.

In some cases, a governmental body or nonprofit agricultural or horticultural organization is not liable for performing, and is not subject to vicarious or contributory liability for another person's performance of, a nondramatic musical work at an annual agricultural or horticultural fair or exhibition. This exemption, however, only applies to performances at an annual fair. It does not apply to Internet broadcasts or transmissions of them.

Performance of a nondramatic literary or musical work in the course of a social function organized and promoted by a nonprofit veterans' organization or a nonprofit fraternal organization to which the general public is not invited is permitted if the proceeds from the performance, after deducting the reasonable costs of producing the performance, are used exclusively for charitable purposes and not for financial gain. This exemption does not apply to the social functions of a college or university fraternity or sorority unless the social function is held solely to raise funds for a specific charitable purpose. It also does not apply to Internet broadcasts or transmissions of the performance.

Performing or displaying copyrighted works during face-to-face teaching activities at a nonprofit educational institution is permissible.

Live performances of musical works and nondramatic literary works are permitted if they are free or if all proceeds are used for charitable, religious or educational purposes. This exemption does not apply to broadcasts or transmissions of the performance.

Performances of nondramatic literary works for blind or deaf persons (i.e., reading aloud, communicating with sign language, etc.) may be transmitted to blind or deaf persons, provided the transmission is not for commercial advantage and is made by a governmental body, a noncommercial educational broadcast station, a radio subcarrier authorization, or a cable system.

Videotaping a television broadcast for viewing at a later time is permitted, so long as it is not done for financial gain. The exemption only authorizes copying and displaying a work at the place where the copy is normally kept. It does not authorize the distribution of copies to others. Nor does it authorize public performance or display of the copy. This exemption does not authorize transmitting a home-taped television broadcast from a website, for example.

A restaurant, bar, retail store or other business establishment may play authorized radio, television, cable and satellite broadcasts or transmissions of nondramatic musical works if it does not charge people to see or hear them. The exemption is subject to detailed conditions relating to the size of the establishment and the size and number of screens or speakers that may be employed. The exemption does not authorize the retransmission of music beyond the establishment where it is received.

A retail establishment that is open to the public may "perform" sound recordings of nondramatic musical works (such as by playing a CD) for the sole purpose of promoting sales of sound recordings or devices used to play them, provided it does not charge people to listen to them. This exemption does not authorize transmission beyond the establishment.

A performance of a dramatic literary work may be transmitted to blind or deaf persons if the work was published at least ten years before the performance, provided the transmission is made by a radio subcarrier authorization and is not for commercial advantage.

A number of exemptions have been carved out for libraries and archives. For example, displaying near its photocopy machine a notice that library materials may be subject to copyright protection will protect a library from contributory liability if an unsupervised patron uses the library's photocopy machine to infringe a copyrighted work. This is just one of several exemptions for libraries and archives. The statutory exemptions do not override any licensing agreements or contracts under which a library has obtained a copy of a work. Thus, if a library obtains software under a license, and the license prohibits something which an exemption appears to permit, then the library must abide by the terms of the license agreement.

The Digital Millennium Copyright Act

Congress has enacted some safe harbors to protect website owners, hosts, and other online service providers from contributory liability for the infringing activity of users of such services.

Applicability

The Digital Millennium Copyright Act (DMCA) only applies to works that are protected by federal copyright law. It does not apply to public domain works, trademarks, privacy rights, etc. Moreover, the DMCA is a U.S. law, so it only protects online service providers in the United States, not service providers situated in other countries.

The DMCA's 4 safe harbors

The DMCA provides safe harbors for four kinds of online activity:

- hosting user-provided content
- providing information location tools (such as search engines and hypertext linking)
- caching
- routing and transmission.

General eligibility requirements

To qualify for any of these safe harbors, a person must meet three general requirements, in addition to any other requirements that may apply to a particular safe harbor:

(1) Be an online service provider;
(2) Implement a policy of terminating the accounts of repeat infringers; and
(c) Refrain from interfering with copyright protection measures.

ONLINE SERVICE PROVIDER

An *online service provider* is "a provider of online services or network access, or the operator of facilities therefore," including "an entity offering the transmission, routing, or providing of connections for digital online communications, between or among points specified by a user, of material of the user's choosing, without modification to the content of the material as sent or received."[13] The definition includes ISPs and those who provide an online service to others. Providing information or entertainment to website visitors is a service. Web hosting services, email services, file-sharing networks, and search engines are also online services, as are online auction services and sites displaying third-party advertising. "'[S]ervice provider' is defined so broadly that we have trouble imagining the existence of an online service that would not fall under the definitions...."[14]

---

[13] 17 U.S.C. § 512(k) (2017).
[14] In re Aimster, 252 F. Supp. 2d 634, 658 (N.D. Ill. 2002), *aff'd*, 334 F.3d 643 (7th

REPEAT INFRINGER TERMINATION POLICY

An online service provider must implement a policy of terminating the accounts of those who use the service to infringe a copyright more than once. The service provider must also inform subscribers and account holders about the repeat infringer policy.

ACCOMMODATION OF COPYRIGHT PROTECTION MEASURES

An online service provider must accommodate, and must not interfere with, any standard technical measures that are used by a copyright owner to identify or protect copyrighted works, if accommodating them does not impose substantial costs on the service provider or substantial burdens on the service provider's system.

User-provided content

17 U.S.C. § 512(c) establishes a set of rules collectively known as notice-and-take-down provisions. It provides that a service provider may not be sued for damages for copyright infringement based on the storage, at the direction of a user, of material that resides on a system or network controlled or operated by or for the service provider, if the service provider qualifies for the protections of the Act and complies with specified procedures for dealing with claims of copyright infringement. An injunction may still be sought against a provider who complies with the DMCA, but monetary damages for contributory infringement may not be recovered.

NO DIRECT FINANCIAL BENEFIT

To receive the benefit of immunity from contributory liability for user-provided content, a service provider must meet the general

---

Cir. 2003).

eligibility requirements and, in addition, must not receive a financial benefit directly attributable to the infringing activity.

No Knowledge of Infringing Content

Eligibility for immunity from contributory liability for user-provided content is lost if the service provider knows or should know, at the time the user posts the material, that it infringes a copyright.

In most cases, an online service provider will not have foreknowledge of the infringing nature of user-provided content because users often share material without first informing the owner what it is they plan to post. If a user gives advance notice of what he intends to post, however, and either tells the owner or it is readily apparent that the content intended to be posted infringes a copyright, then the DMCA will not protect the owner who then proceeds to authorize the post.

No Solicitation or Inducement

A service provider is not immune from contributory liability for user-provided content if s/he actively induces, encourages or solicits users of the service to post material to the site that s/he knows or reasonably should know are likely to infringe a copyright.

Copyright Notifications Agent

An online service provider who wants to enjoy the safe harbor the DMCA provides for user-provided content must designate an agent to receive notifications of claimed infringement. She must also let people know who the agent is and where to send notices of claimed infringement. The designation must be made online at www.copyright.gov.

Prompt Removal Upon Receiving Notice of Infringing Content

An online service provider must promptly remove or disable access to material that is claimed to infringe a copyright upon learning of the infringement or claimed infringement. Otherwise, the DMCA will not insulate the provider from contributory liability for publishing the content. A provider is bound by this requirement, however, only if the notification is in proper form and properly served.

Counter Notifications

The user who provided the content that an online service provider has removed in response to a take-down notice may file a counter notification asserting that the material does not, in fact, infringe a copyright.

A service provider is exempt from liability for removing or disabling access to a content provider's material only if:

- The material was removed or access to it was disabled in good faith;
- It was done in response to a notification of claimed copyright infringement, or is based on facts or circumstances from which infringement is apparent;
- The service provider took reasonable steps promptly to notify the content provider that it has removed or disabled access to it;
- The service provider promptly provided the person who served the notification of claimed infringement with a copy of the counter notification;
- The service provider promptly informed the person who served the notification of infringement that it will replace the removed material or cease disabling access to it in ten business days;
- The service provider restored the removed material (or ceased disabling access to it) not less than ten, nor more than fourteen, business days following receipt of the counter notice, unless its designated agent first received notice from the person who submitted the notification of claimed copyright infringement that such person has filed an action seeking a court order to restrain the content provider from engaging in infringing activity relating to the material on the service provider's system or network.

If a service provider complies with all DMCA requirements, then she will be protected from liability to the copyright claimant and also from liability to the content provider.

MISREPRESENTATION

Knowingly making false or misleading statements of fact in a notification or counter-notification may result in liability for damages, attorney fees and costs.[15] The DMCA also provides a civil cause of action for the recovery of compensatory damages, including attorney fees and costs, against a person who knowingly misrepresents that material or activity was removed or disabled by mistake or misidentification. Making a false statement in a DMCA notice is also punishable as perjury.

Information location tools

17 U.S.C. § 512(d) provides qualified immunity from contributory liability for online service providers that provide information location tools (such as search engines, directories or hypertext links) to refer, direct or connect users to infringing content on other websites. In addition to satisfying the general eligibility requirements, a website owner must meet also meet three additional eligibility requirements:

- no knowledge of infringing activity;
- either no right or ability to control the infringing activity, or no direct financial benefit from the infringing activity; and
- prompt removal upon receiving proper notification of claimed infringement.

[15] 17 U.S.C. § 512 (2017).

Caching

Caching is the temporary storage of recently accessed Web content. The DMCA protects eligible online service providers from liability for creating cached copies of web pages.

Routing and transmission

The DMCA provides a safe harbor from copyright infringement liability for service providers that operate as nothing more than passive conduits for other people's communications. To qualify, the service must be truly passive. Because most website owners have some level of supervisory power over user-provided content, this safe harbor does not often apply.

Circumvention of copyright protection measures

The anti-circumvention provisions of the DMCA broadly prohibit the circumvention of technological measures that people have been taken to prevent access to, or copying of, a copyrighted work. The DMCA also prohibits making, importing, selling or transferring devices or services that are marketed or primarily used to circumvent copyright protection measures. Knowingly linking to a site that traffics in copyright circumvention devices or services is also prohibited. Some limited exceptions apply, such circumvention for law enforcement, encryption research, security testing, protection of privacy and/or minors, or reverse engineering by a lawful owner of a copy.

Copyright management information

Copyright management information is information about the work, the author, the copyright owner, and if applicable, the performer, writer or director; the terms and conditions for use of the work; and any other information the Register of Copyrights may prescribe.

Tampering with or removing copyright management information is prohibited, as is distributing copies of products that have been tampered with or that have had such information improperly removed from them. Both civil remedies and criminal penalties are available to enforce this provision.

Transfers

Transfers of ownership of a copyright may be voluntary or involuntary. Copyrights are potentially subject to seizure by creditors for the satisfaction of unpaid debts, in much the same way that other kinds of property are. A unit of government may not seize a copyright.

Upon a copyright owner's death, title to the copyright passes to the heirs of her estate or, if she had a will, then to the beneficiary designated in the will.

Voluntary transfers that occur during the owner's lifetime are called *assignments.*

Beginning in 1978, a signed writing is required for an assignment of copyright ownership. Assignments that were effected before 1978 may be either oral or written.

Recording an assignment is not required. Failing to do so does not affect the validity of the transfer, and it is no longer a prerequisite to filing an infringement lawsuit in court. It can help protect an assignee from losing rights to another person to whom the copyright owner might have assigned rights in the same work. It provides strong evidentiary support for the existence and date of the assignment. Also, if the document clearly identifies the work and the work has been registered, then recording an assignment gives the whole world constructive notice of all the facts stated in the assignment.

Under the Copyright Act, a transfer is effective as against a competing claimant of another alleged transfer of the same copyright if it is (a) executed first, and (b) recorded either one month after its execution in the United States (two months, if executed in another country) or before the other alleged transfer is recorded.

A later transferee who gives valuable consideration for the transfer, without notice of the previous transfer, will prevail against a previous transferee if the previous transferee neither recorded the transfer within one month (two months, if executed in another country) nor recorded it before the later transferee did.

The rule applies to "transfers" of copyrights, as that term is defined in the Copyright Act. This includes both outright assignments and grants of exclusive licenses. It also includes grants of security interests in copyrights. It does not include grants of nonexclusive licenses.

Licenses

Any of the exclusive rights of a copyright owner (reproduction, distribution, public display, public performance, digital transmission, making derivative works) may be licensed to others.

The Copyright Act blurs the distinction between transfers and licenses a bit by referring to grants of exclusive licenses, as well as assignments, as "transfers of copyright ownership":

> A "transfer of copyright ownership" is an assignment, mortgage, exclusive license, or any other conveyance, alienation, or hypothecation of a copyright or of any of the exclusive rights comprised in a copyright, whether or not it is limited in time or place of effect, but not including a nonexclusive license.[16391]

In copyright law, then, a grant of an exclusive license to exercise one or more of the rights of copyright ownership (distribution, performance, etc.) transfers "ownership" of that right, which may be subject to terms and conditions that are spelled out in the license agreement. An exclusive license does not transfer ownership of the title to the copyright, however.

---

16 17 U.S.C. § 101 (2017).

The explanation for this unusual and confusing language is that Congress wanted to make it possible for exclusive licensees to avail themselves of certain legal benefits of copyright ownership that licensees ordinarily do not possess. This includes the rights to commence a lawsuit against an infringer and to apply for registration of the copyright.

A grant of an exclusive license, then, is not really a transfer of ownership; the licensee is just entitled to be treated like one for purposes of enforcing the copyright.

Before 1978, licenses could be oral or written. Exclusive licenses granted after 1977 must be in writing and signed by the copyright owner. A nonexclusive license may be written or oral, unless a writing is required under the applicable contract law of a state. A written transfer terminates all prior oral licenses.

Recordation

Recording a license is optional. A license is enforceable between the parties even if it has not been recorded. If the document clearly identifies the work and the work has been registered, though, then recording a license gives the whole world constructive notice of all the facts stated in the license document.

Divisibility of rights

The rights that are bundled in a copyright—reproduction, distribution, public display, public performance, digital transmission, making derivative works—may be unbundled and transferred either separately or with other rights. For example, a performance right may be transferred without also transferring a right to make derivative works; distribution rights may be transferred without also transferring the right to make derivative works; and so on.

Exclusive vs. non-exclusive licenses

A license may be either exclusive or nonexclusive. A nonexclusive license gives the licensee permission to use the work but does not give the licensee the right to exclude others from using the work. An exclusive license not only gives the licensee permission to use the work, but also confers the right to exclude everyone else – even the author – from using it. An exclusive licensee of one or more of the exclusive rights of copyright ownership has standing to file an infringement claim and apply for registration of the copyright.

Effect on other intellectual property rights

A grant of a license to use a copyrighted work does not confer a license to use a trademark or patent, and vice versa. Accordingly, if a work that is the subject of a copyright license is also a trademark or the subject of a patent (as sometimes happens in the case of computer programs), the copyright licensing agreement should address the question whether and to what extent rights in those properties are also being licensed for use.

Copyright is also distinct from the rights of visual artists under the Visual Artists Rights Act. Because those rights are not transferable, a copyright license or assignment will not be effective to transfer them even if the agreement purports to do so.

Music and sound recording licenses

Kinds of licenses

The 5 principal kinds of licenses for musical works and sound recordings are:

- Folio
- Performance

- Mechanical
- Master use
- Synchronization

A *folio* license is a license to publish sheet music or the tablature for a musical work.

A *performance* license is a license to publicly perform a musical work or sound recording. A *mechanical* license is a license to make and distribute copies of a musical work.

A *master use* license is a license to make and distribute copies of a sound recording.

A *synchronization* license is a license to use music in combination with another work, such as a video.

Copyrights in a sound recording and in the musical or literary work performed on it are different things. If permission is sought to publicly perform or transmit a recording of a song, then two licenses will be needed: one for the sound recording and one for the musical or literary work performed on it.

Licensing musical works

FOLIO LICENSES

Folio licenses are obtained by negotiation with the owner of the copyright in the musical work or the owner's agent. There is no compulsory or statutory license to publish sheet music, tablature or lyrics.

PERFORMANCE LICENSES

Performance rights agencies like ASCAP and BMI handle licensing of musical works for many songwriters. These agencies license the right to publicly perform musical works at concerts, in radio or television broadcasts, as background music in bars, restaurants and retail stores, for music-on-hold services, and for transmissions via the Internet. They do not handle folio licenses or mechanical licenses.

A performance license does not confer authority to make digital files of the performance available for download on a website, or to sell or give away copies of a recording of the performance. A performance rights licensing agreement does not include the right to make derivative works, such as arrangements, unless the contract so provides.

A performance license may be needed for noninteractive streaming of music on the Internet. Because interactive streaming (where a user can listen on demand) is functionally similar to both the performance of a musical work and the delivery of a copy of it to the user, both a performance license and a mechanical license may be needed. The performance license may be obtainable through ASCAP or another performance rights agency, but a mechanical license is not.

A compulsory license is one that is established by law when certain conditions are met. There is no compulsory license for performance rights in a musical work. A compulsory license might exist for recording and distributing copies of a musical composition, but not for performing it.

Performance rights licensing agencies set their own rates and terms. Usually, the royalty is calculated as a percentage of the licensee's revenue, but an agency may, in the alternative, offer a blanket license for the use of multiple songs for a specified fee.

Mechanical licenses

A mechanical license is needed to make and distribute copies of a performance of a copyrighted musical work. This is true whether the copies are physical or digital downloads. Interactive streaming is functionally equivalent to distributing a copy, albeit only for a limited time, so it arguably requires both a performance license and a mechanical license. A mechanical license is not needed for noninteractive streaming.

The Harry Fox Agency is the primary agency for the mechanical licensing of musical works. It handles licenses to make and distribute physical copies (e.g., CDs) as well as ringtones and digital downloads. It handles both voluntary and compulsory licenses. It does not handle performance rights. A person who is interested in obtaining a mechanical license for a musical work is not required to work with the Harry Fox Agency. Licenses may also be obtained in two other ways: negotiation with the copyright owner (or his agent) directly, or by invoking and satisfying the requirements for a compulsory license.

Compulsory Licenses

A compulsory license is a statutory license to make and distribute copies of a musical work. It is a license that the Copyright Act automatically grants to anyone who wants to record and distribute a performance of a song even if the copyright owner does not consent to it—provided certain conditions are met. Basically, it is the right to record and distribute a performance of a cover version of another person's copyrighted musical composition.

The compulsory license only applies to the right to record a musical work and then distribute copies of the recording. It does not include a right to publicly perform the song. A compulsory license also does not confer synchronization rights.

A compulsory license is subject to certain conditions, limitations and exclusions:

- There is no compulsory license for dramatic works
- At least one recording authorized by the copyright owner must already have been made. This ensures that songwriters have the first shot at exploiting their works commercially No alteration of the basic melody or fundamental character of the work is allowed (a license to make a derivative work would be needed for that)
- Notice must be sent to the copyright owner before any copies are distributed, and not later than thirty days after the recording is made
- A royalty must be paid

- Periodic accountings are required
- Distribution must be limited to members of the public for their personal use.

A compulsory license does not include a right to make and distribute copies for use in background music systems, jukeboxes, broadcasting, or other public uses.

A person seeking a compulsory license must serve written notice of intention to obtain a compulsory license on the owner of the copyright in the musical work or her agent.

If Copyright Office records do not identify the copyright owner(s), or do not include an address at which notice can be served, then the notice may instead be filed with the Copyright Office.

A separate notice must be served for each musical work for which a compulsory license is sought.

Failure to timely and properly serve a Notice of Intention forecloses the possibility of a compulsory license.

Also, there is no compulsory license to make and distribute copies of a musical work unless a copyright owner is identified in a registration or some other record that has been filed with the Copyright Office.

A compulsory license includes a license to make a new arrangement of a musical work without need for the copyright owner's permission, provided it does not change the basic melody or the fundamental character of the work. Unless the copyright owner agrees, however, a compulsory licensee does not acquire a copyright in the arrangement.

If the copyright owner is identified in Copyright Office records, then a compulsory licensee must pay a specified royalty to the copyright owner, but only for any recordings that are made and distributed after Copyright Office records first identified the copyright owner. A compulsory licensee must maintain accounting records showing how the royalty was calculated for each work. Accounting statements must contain information specified by the Register of Copyrights.

If a licensee fails to provide a monthly or annual accounting statement, the copyright owner may give written notice to the licensee that if the default is not cured within thirty days from the date of notice, the compulsory license will be automatically terminated. Thereafter, any further sale or distribution of copies for which royalties have not been made is actionable as copyright infringement.

Licensing sound recordings

PERFORMANCE LICENSES

Copyright protection for sound recordings first began in 1972. It was initially limited to an exclusive right to copy, distribute and make derivative works. There was no exclusive public performance right for sound recordings. So long as they paid a licensing fee for the musical work, radio and television broadcasters could freely play recorded song performances on the air without infringing a sound recording copyright.

At the time, this made sense. Radio broadcasts were noninteractive. Listeners had no control over what they played. If they wanted the ability to listen to a particular song at any time they chose, then they had to buy a copy of the recording. Recording artists and record companies made their money from sales of physical copies of their recordings in the form of record albums and cassette tapes. Radio stations provided free advertising for record companies. Since they were getting free advertising, it made no sense for record companies and recording artists to object, much less to expect to be paid a royalty.

The Internet changed that model, introducing many new ways of delivering music to listeners. An Internet website can be set up to operate like a traditional radio broadcasting company; it can be set up to operate like a music store; it can be set up to operate like a block party where everybody brings their own copies of records to play for each other; it can be set up to operate like a trading club where people exchange copies of their records with each other; or it can be set up to operate like a pirating operation where people make unauthorized copies of records and sell or give them away to other people. It also can be set up to do more than one of these things.

Streaming, in particular, created a thorny legal issue. It is like a radio broadcast in that it involves a performance of a sound recording. If a user has some control over which songs to play, though, then it is like a distribution of a copy. Making songs available for interactive streaming from a website displaces the need to purchase a copy of the recording.

Record companies lobbied Congress for a performance right in sound recording copyrights. In 1995, Congress responded by enacting the Digital Performance Right in Sound Recordings Act[402] (DPRA). This law gives the owner of a copyright in a sound recording an exclusive right to digitally perform it. The DMCA refined the DPRA by establishing categories for different kinds of digital transmissions, each with different associated performance rights, statutory licensing requirements, and royalty rates.

The DMCA's elaborate system of statutory licensing represents a compromise between the interests of Internet-based companies and the interests of record companies. In striking this compromise, Congress attempted to implement a system similar to the one for nondigital sound recordings. Like a music store, a distributor of digital downloads or interactive streams must secure the permission of the copyright owner. Like radio and television broadcasts, noninteractive digital transmissions may occur without the permission of the owner of the copyright in the sound recording. An Internet broadcaster may invoke a statutory license instead of negotiating with the copyright owner for permission. Unlike radio and television broadcasts, however, a noninteractive digital transmission may require the payment of a small royalty to the owner of the copyright in the sound recording in some cases.

A website offering interactive streaming or downloads of sound recordings cannot invoke a statutory license. The permission of the owners of the copyrights in the sound recordings must be obtained.

Unlike the royalty that is required to be paid in the case of a statutory license, the royalty is arrived at by negotiation between the copyright owner and the website owner.

The only new exclusive right the DPRA establishes for owners of sound recording copyrights is the right to digitally perform (transmit) the recording. It does not give sound recording copyright owners an exclusive right to publicly perform the recording in other ways, such as by means of a traditional radio station broadcast.

Statutory Licenses for Noninteractive Transmissions

The Copyright Act establishes licenses to use certain kinds of copyrighted works, provided the conditions specified in the Act are satisfied. These are called *statutory* licenses because they are provided for by statute; the copyright owner's consent is not required. A compulsory license to record a cover version of a musical work is an example of a statutory license. The Act also establishes statutory licenses for certain noninteractive transmissions of sound recordings.

In situations where there is no negotiated royalty agreement, royalty rates are determined and set by the Copyright Royalty Board. The Board also establishes requirements for statutory licensees to give reasonable notice and keep adequate records of their use of a sound recording pursuant to a statutory license.

The royalties to be paid pursuant to a statutory license may not be used as a basis for reducing the amount of any royalty payable to the owner of the copyright in the musical or literary work.

SoundExchange is a sound recording performance rights administrator that collects and disburses statutory license royalty payments from digital transmitters to record companies and recording artists. It does not manage royalties payable to the owners of copyrights in musical or literary works.

The royalty rate that is set by the Copyright Board for statutory licenses to use sound recordings is adjusted annually.

VOLUNTARY LICENSES FOR NONINTERACTIVE TRANSMISSIONS

If no exemption or statutory license applies to a copyright-protected sound recording, use of it will require a license that is voluntarily granted by the copyright owner. To ensure fair competition, Congress has provided that if an owner of a copyright in a sound recording grants an affiliated entity a license to digitally transmit the recording, then it must make a license available, on no less favorable terms, to all bona fide entities that offer similar services.

An *affiliated entity* is an entity that engages in noninteractive transmissions and in which the sound recording copyright licensor has a direct or indirect ownership or partnership interest of 5% or more of the outstanding voting or nonvoting stock.

EXCLUSIVE LICENSES FOR INTERACTIVE TRANSMISSIONS

Interactive digital transmissions are not subject to statutory licensing. There are, however, some statutory limitations on a sound recording copyright owners' freedom of contract when licensing interactive streaming rights. These are intended to promote competition and to prevent the monopolization of performance rights in sound recordings, as well as to ensure the existence of more than one outlet for online interactive streaming to consumers.

MASTER USE LICENSES

A website owner selling digital downloads or physical copies of music recordings will need a mechanical license for the musical work and a master use license for the sound recording. The compulsory license provided in 17 U.S.C. § 115 to make and distribute copies of a musical work does not include a right to make and distribute copies of the sound recording. And statutory licenses available under 17 U.S.C. § 114 generally are for streaming, not the distribution of digital downloads or copies. The owner of the sound recording copyright will be liable to the owner of the copyright in the musical work for a third party's transmission of the sound recording with the musical work in it only if the sound recording copyright owner specifically licensed distribution rights in the musical work to the third party. A website that transmits either work without a valid license will be liable in any event.

MUSIC VIDEOS

A person wishing to make a music video by combining a performance of a song with a video will need a synchronization license. Performing rights agencies normally do not handle synchronization licensing. Instead, it is necessary to negotiate a licensing agreement with the owners of the copyrights in the musical composition, the sound recording of it, and the audiovisual work—to the extent the person making the music video is not the owner of the copyright(s) in these elements.

The Musical Works Modernization Act

In October, 2018, the Musical Works Modernization Act[407] (MWMA) was signed into law. It changes the way compulsory licenses to reproduce and distribute nondramatic musical works are obtained. The requirements for obtaining a compulsory license to make and distribute copies nonelectronically (e.g., CDs or other physical copies) remain intact. A person seeking a compulsory license to make and distribute copies of a nondramatic musical work digitally (such as digital downloads or interactive streaming), however may no longer file notices of intention to obtain compulsory licenses with the Copyright Office, even if the copyright owner's identity and/or address are not available. Beginning in 2021, licenses to make and distribute music digitally are obtained by sending a Notice of License to a mechanical licensing collective (MLC). The MLC issues blanket licenses. It also collects and distributes royalties, and identifies musical works and their owners for payment. It is to establish and maintain a publicly accessible database of musical works and, to the extent known, the identity and location of the copyright owners and the sound recordings in which the musical works are embodied. Operational costs of the MLC will be paid for by digital music providers, in part by means of an administrative assessment. In the interim, digital music providers are shielded from liability for failing to serve a compulsory notice license on a copyright owner, provided they can demonstrate that they engaged in a good faith, commercially reasonable effort to identify and locate the copyright owner. Accrued royalties must be paid if and when a copyright owner is located, however. The MWMA also changes the method by which copyright royalty judges set rates.

Author's Right to Terminate Transfers

Copyright assignments and licenses are subject to a statutory rule unique to copyright law. The Copyright Act of 1976 gives authors (or their heirs) an inalienable right to terminate transfers (assignments or licenses) of the copyrights in their works, for any reason or for no reason at all, under certain circumstances. The termination must be in writing and served on the transferee in order to be effective. It must comply with Copyright Office regulations and be recorded. It must be served between two and ten years before the effective date of the termination.

The termination right does not apply to works made for hire. Also, the right may not be exercised to terminate a testamentary transfer.

If an author exercises this right, however, the transferee may nevertheless continue to exploit derivative works produced under the transfer prior to the termination. The terminated transferee may not make new derivative works without permission, though.

The specific contours of the termination right vary depending on whether the transfer was made before January 1, 1978 or not.

PRE-1978 TRANSFERS

The author (or his statutory heirs) may terminate a pre-1978 transfer of a renewal term interest to the extent of the thirty-nine-year extension of the renewal term that Congress granted (the nineteen-year extension granted in the 1976 Act plus the twenty-year extension granted in the Sonny Bono Copyright Term Extension Act of 1998). If an author (or his heirs) does not exercise the right with respect to the initial nineteen-year term extension, there is a second opportunity to exercise the right to recapture the twenty-year term extension. The rights must be exercised within the time periods specified in Sections 304(c) and (d) of the Copyright Act.

POST-1977 TRANSFERS

An author may terminate a post-1977 transfer of a copyright during the 5-year period beginning at the end of 35 years after the transfer. If the transfer included a transfer of the right of publication, however, then the five-year period begins at the earlier of 35 years after publication or 40 years after the transfer was made

This right belongs only to the author or, if the author is deceased, the statutory heirs specified in the Copyright Act. With the exception of heirs who have a statutory right to terminate as provided in the Copyright Act, a transferee of the copyright from the author does not have a termination right. In the case of a joint work, a termination is effective only if a majority of the joint authors join in it.

3 TRADEMARKS

A trademark identifies the source of a product or service, distinguishing the product or service from those of others.

Sources of law

Trademarks are governed by state, federal and international laws. The Lanham Act is the primary source of federal trademark law in the United States. At the state level, common law is the principal source. Many states have enacted statutes to supplement or modify the common law.

Kinds of trademarks

A trademark can consist of nearly anything that is perceptible—words, phrases, symbols, drawings, photographs, graphic designs, colors, shapes, sounds, motions, scents, textures, product design, packaging, architecture, interior design. If it can be used in commerce to identify the source of goods or services and to distinguish them from the goods or services of others, it has the potential to be a trademark.

The principal categories are:

- standard character ("word mark")
- design
- sound
- shape
- color
- scent
- texture
- motion.

A trademark for services is also known as a *service mark*. A trademark indicating membership in an organization is called a *collective membership mark*. A trademark indicating approval by an organization is called a *certification mark*. There is no special term for a trademark for goods. They are simply called *trademarks*. Unless the context otherwise requires, references to trademarks include all of these kinds of trademarks, not just trademarks for goods.

Trademarks can also be classified as either:

- labels; or
- trade dress

Trade dress refers to the packaging or design of the product or of the place where a service is provided).

Standard character marks

Standard character marks consist of letter(s) and/or word(s) in Latin characters; number(s) in Roman or Arabic numerals; common punctuation or diacritical marks; and any combination(s) of any of these. Although names and short phrases are not protected by copyright, they may be protected as trademarks.

Designs

A design trademark is a logo, drawing, photographic, or some other visual graphic.

Sounds

Sounds and sound combinations can serve as trademarks if they are used to identify the source of goods or services. The sound must be nonfunctional, however. A buzzing sound, for example, cannot be used as a trademark for a brand of alarm clocks because buzzing sounds serve the function of waking people up.

Colors

Colors and color combinations can be trademarks. For example, the color brown, as used in connection with parcel delivery services, is a UPS trademark. They are not considered inherently distinctive however. Therefore, in order to claim trademark rights in a color or color combination, it is necessary to establish that it has acquired secondary meaning, i.e., that consumers have come to associate it with a particular business, product or service.

Colors, too, must be nonfunctional. If the color helps identify the flavor of a product, or makes it more desirable, then it serves an aesthetic function, and therefore does not receive trademark protection. If the color improves the visibility of a product as to which visibility is an important characteristic (e.g., the blaze orange used in clothing for safety while hunting), then it is not a protectable trademark.

Scents, textures, flavors

Textures, scents and flavors sometimes receive trademark protection. They are not protected, however, if they serve a useful function other than identifying the source of the product. For this reason, a flavor that makes a food or drug product more palatable, or an antiperspirant pleasant to smell, does not get trademark protection. Similarly, because the bumpy texture of a soft drink bottle gives the holder a better grip, it is not protected by trademark.

Flavors, scents and textures are not inherently distinctive, so proof of secondary meaning is necessary in order to claim trademark rights in them. Some courts, however, hold that a scent may be inherently distinctive if it is used in connection with completely unrelated goods. A citrus scent for biofuels is an example.

Trademark rights cannot be claimed in naturally occurring flavors.

Motions

Motions may be protectable as trademarks. The Peabody Hotels' March of the Peabody Ducks is an example.

Trade dress

The shape, size, color(s), texture or design of a product or its packaging is called *trade dress*. Sales techniques and the architecture, lighting and/or decor of a place where a service is performed are also kinds of trade dress. If they serve as distinctive source identifiers, then they may be protected trademarks. Trademark rights, however, cannot be claimed in advantageous functional aspects of a product, service, packaging or presentation.

Requirements

The four essential requirements for a valid trademark in the United States are:

- Use in commerce
- Non-functionality

- Distinctiveness
- No likelihood of confusion.

Use in commerce

In the United States, trademark rights arise through use. A trademark may exist and be enforced even if it is unregistered. In fact, it is not possible to create trademark rights in the United States merely by registering a mark with a trademark office. It is necessary to actually use the mark in commerce.

A *common law trademark* is a one that arises through a person's use of it. A *registered trademark* is one that has been registered with a government agency, typically the USPTO. In the United States, all registered trademarks are also common law trademarks, but not all common law trademarks are registered.

Because use in commerce is required, merely having an idea for a brand name, logo, etc. is not enough to give rise to any protectable trademark rights, even if the idea is written down, drawn on paper, or recorded in some other way.

Domain name registration is not sufficient, by itself, to establish trademark rights. The use must be in connection with particular goods or services. Standing alone, a business name, logo, etc. is not a trademark. It can become a trademark only if and when it is used in association with particular goods or services. This might happen when it is affixed to goods or packaging, displayed with goods or services in some other way, or otherwise made known to purchasers in the ordinary course of business in a way that associates the mark with particular goods or services.

In the case of a service mark, affixing a label is impractical. For a service mark, therefore, displaying a sign at the place where services are provided, or on letterhead or in advertising material, may suffice as "use in commerce," provided services are also actually rendered.

The use must be substantial, not trivial. It must also be continuous. Sporadic use is not enough. De minimis, inconsequential use (use that is so minimal that it is not likely to come to the attention of a competitor) does not qualify. Purely internal sales or transfers (such as sales limited to employees of the business that is selling the product) do not qualify, either. Shipments of labeled prototypes to a prospective manufacturer do not qualify, but shipments of labeled products to a laboratory for testing might.

The commercial transaction must be bona fide. A sale that is made solely for the purpose of preserving trademark rights is not bona fide. Token use, meaning a single sale bearing no relationship to a plan for commercially exploiting the mark, does not qualify as bona fide. Multiple sales of the goods or services to consumers normally qualify as bona fide. Sales in a test market do, too.

Finally, the use must have the purpose or effect of identifying the source of goods or services. It is not necessary that a mark have the effect of identifying the specific name of the trademark owner. FRESCA, for example, is a valid trademark whether people realize the product is manufactured and sold by the Coca-Cola Company or not.

Priority of Use

In the United States, the first to use a trademark in commerce in a geographic area acquires exclusive right to use it there.

The use must be in connection with the sale, lease or licensing of a product or service. Presale advertisements and new product announcements do not qualify.

Uses occurring prior to the establishment of a valid trademark are disregarded. This means that if a mark is not inherently distinctive, i.e., if it is merely descriptive, then the first use will not be deemed to occur until after the mark has acquired distinctiveness. A mark that must rely on secondary meaning in order to be distinctive does not come into existence as a trademark until the secondary meaning has become associated with it in consumers' minds.

Under the Paris Convention, if a citizen of a member country files a trademark application in his own country, and then files an application in another member country within six months, then the priority of both marks is determined by the priority given the mark in connection with the first application.

Non-functionality

An exclusive right to use a feature of a product that enhances its value is a kind of advantage that could result in the acquisition of monopoly power. Trademark law protects fair competition, not the acquisition of monopoly power. Accordingly, functional aspects of a product or service, that is to say, features that enhance a product's usefulness, are not given trademark protection.

There are two kinds of functionality: *de facto* and *de jure*. A feature of a product or its packaging is de facto functional when it performs an essential function of the product. It is de jure functional when it serves an advantageous purpose (other than brand distinctiveness) even though it may not be necessary for the essential functions of the product.

Functionality is likely to be an issue with respect to trade dress. Color would seem, at first glance, to be a nonfunctional aspect of an outboard boat motor, for example. It certainly has no de facto functionality in relation to the essential purposes of a boat motor. Nor does the cost of paint vary much by color. An outboard motor will power a boat as efficiently and at about the same cost whether it is painted green or black. In *Brunswick Corp. v. British Seagull Ltd.*,[17336] however, a court held that the black color of an outboard boat motor has de jure functionality. Why? Because black is compatible with more boat color schemes than other colors are. Also, black makes motors look smaller. These things give black motors an aesthetic edge in consumer sales that is unrelated to brand loyalty. Trademark protection cannot be afforded to black outboard motors because preventing competitors from using black as the color of their motors would put them at an unfair competitive disadvantage.

---

[17] 35 F.3d 1527, 1531 (Fed. Cir. 1994).

Distinctiveness

To receive trademark protection, a mark must be distinctive. It must stand out in such a way that consumers associate it with a particular source of the goods or services. A SHOES label on a box of shoes gives a consumer no idea who made them or where they are from. It does associate the shoes with a particular source, and it does not do anything to distinguish them from shoes that are made and sold by other companies.

There are two kinds of distinctiveness:

- Inherent
- Acquired.

Distinctiveness may be inherent or acquired. An *inherently distinctive* mark is one that requires no further explanation to understand that it could only be used as an identifier of the source of particular goods or services. A very distinctive mark is called a *strong* mark.

A mark that is not inherently distinctive but comes to be associated in consumers' minds with a particular source is said to have to have *acquired distinctiveness*. A mark that is not inherently distinctive does not receive trademark protection unless it has acquired *secondary meaning* as a source identifier of a particular product or service.

Not all packaging is inherently distinctive, but it can be. Product design, on the other hand, always requires proof of secondary meaning in order to meet the distinctiveness requirement.

Under the Lanham Act, continuous, exclusive use of a mark for five years is prima facie evidence of secondary meaning. Evidence may be introduced to establish a different period of time.

THE DOCTRINE OF FOREIGN EQUIVALENTS

The doctrine of foreign equivalents is the rule that the distinctiveness of foreign words and expressions is to be evaluated after the words have been translated into English.

THE 5 LEVELS OF DISTINCTIVENESS

There are five levels of distinctiveness. From strongest to weakest, they are:

- Fanciful
- Arbitrary
- Suggestive
- Descriptive
- Generic.[18]

A **fanciful** mark is one that has been invented. It has no other meanings. Fanciful marks are inherently strong. They automatically meet the distinctiveness requirement.

An **arbitrary** mark is one which has not been invented, and which does have at least one other meaning, but is used in connection with goods or services to which it bears no reasonable relation. GORILLA glue is an example. Arbitrary marks are also deemed inherently distinctive.

A **suggestive** mark is one that implies something about a product or service without directly describing it. It is like a descriptive mark, except that it "requires imagination, thought and perception to reach a conclusion as to the nature of the goods."[19] JAGUAR, as a trademark for automobiles, is an example of a suggestive mark. A jaguar is an animal with the ability to run fast. The word *jaguar,* however, is not simply a synonym for *fast.* Using this word in connection with an automobile, though, could lead a thinking person to infer that the car is fast. For this reason, it is classified as a suggestive mark rather than a descriptive one. Suggestive marks are inherently distinctive.

A **descriptive** mark is one that directly describes a quality or characteristic of the goods or services, such as their origin, properties,

[18] Abercrombie & Fitch Co. v. Hunting World, 537 F.2d 4 (2d Cir. 1976).

[19] Stix Prods., Inc. v United Merchants & Manufacturers, Inc., 295 F. Supp. 479, 488 (S.D.N.Y. 1968).

ingredients, likely users, who is selling them, etc. JIFFY LUBE is an example. Self-aggrandizing words, like THE BEST, also fall into the descriptive marks category. Descriptive marks do not get trademark protection unless they are shown to have acquired secondary meaning.

Minor alterations or misspellings of descriptive words will not suffice to transform them into fanciful or arbitrary marks.

A description need not be accurate in order to be classified as a descriptive mark. For example, RELIABLE could serve as a trademark for Ford if consumers somehow came to associate that term with the Ford brand. Note, however, that deceptive marks are not protected even if they have secondary meaning.

Generic marks are common, everyday words that are used to identify a kind or category of product or service. Because they are inherently incapable of identifying source, they do not receive any trademark protection at all. The best way to determine whether a term is generic or not is to ask whether its significance to the consumer is the product, not the producer. If consumers use the term as a synonym for the product category regardless of manufacturer identity, then it is generic. MILK, TOYS, LUMBER are examples of generic marks.

A mark that would otherwise be a protected trademark can become an unprotected generic term if enough people regularly use it as a generic term for the category of a product rather than as a particular brand of a product within the category. When this happens, trademark protection is said to have been lost through *genericide*. Some examples of marks that have lost trademark protection through genericide include: ASPIRIN, CELLOPHANE, DRY ICE, ESCALATOR, LAUNDROMAT, SHREDDED WHEAT, THERMOS, TRAMPOLINE, and VIDEOTAPE. This is one reason why it is important to police trademarks to ensure they are being used as brand names and not in a way that could lead to genericide.

Because of the doctrine of foreign equivalents, a foreign word for a generic term will be considered just as generic as the English word is. VINO, for example, is generic as a trademark for wine because it is simply the Italian word for wine.

Likelihood of confusion

A mark receives no protection under trademark law if it is confusingly similar to a mark that is already being used in connection with the same or related goods or services. It does not matter whether the existing mark has been registered or not. Marketing goods or services using a mark that is confusingly similar to a competitor's amounts to unfair competition and trademark infringement.

The general rule is that likelihood of confusion exists if and only if:

- The marks are identical or similar; and
- Either:
    - (i) the goods or services are related in a way that consumers are likely to infer that they come from the same source, or
    - (ii) one of the marks is a famous or well-known one.

Factors relevant to likelihood of confusion include:

- Similarity in appearance, sound, meaning, and/or commercial impression
- Actual consumer confusion
- Length of concurrent use without actual confusion
- Extent of potential confusion
- Similarity of marketing channels
- Similarity of the goods or services
- Degree of care likely to be exercised by a purchaser of the goods or services
- Fame of the preexisting mark
- Number and nature of similar marks in use on similar goods
- Commercial relationship between the owners of the two marks
- Variety of goods on which a mark is used
- Extent to which the subsequent user of the mark can exclude others
- Any other relevant fact.

These are sometimes referred to as the *du Pont* factors, after the case in which they were enunciated, *In re E. I. du Pont de Nemours & Co.*[20]

The Ninth Circuit Court of Appeals has enunciated a modified set of factors:

- Strength of the mark
- Use of the mark on the same, similar or related goods or services
- Similarity of the marks
- Actual confusion
- Intent (reason for choosing the mark)
- Similarity of marketing/advertising channels
- Purchaser's degree of care
- Product line expansion.

These are sometimes called the *Sleekcraft* factors, after the case in which they were enunciated, *AMF Inc. v. Sleekcraft Boats.*[21]

To these lists may be added:

- Consent agreement, if any
- Seriousness of harm to consumers that may result from confusion
- Any other relevant factors.

Consumer surveys are commonly used to establish likelihood of confusion, but they are not the only kinds of evidence. Evidence of actual confusion, although not necessary to succeed on a trademark infringement claim, can help establish likelihood of confusion. Conversely, evidence of long use of both marks without actual confusion can be used as evidence that confusion is unlikely.

Even if trade dress is not serving as a trademark, evidence of similarities in trade dress can be used to help establish a claim of

---

[20] 476 F.2d 1357 (C.C.P.A. 1973).

[21] 599 F.2d 341, 348–349 (9th Cir. 1979).

likelihood of confusion. The nature and quality of the goods or services can also be relevant.

No proof of intent to infringe is necessary to prevail on a claim of trademark infringement. On the other hand, evidence of bad faith intent to infringe can help establish likelihood of confusion. Doing a trademark search and relying on an attorney's opinion can go a long way toward defending against a claim of bad faith intent. By the same token, disregarding the advice of counsel might evidence bad faith intent.

The confusion that is relevant to an infringement claim is confusion as to the source, endorsement or sponsorship of particular goods or services. It must be assessed with reference to the target audience. Goods and services for children must be assessed on the basis of whether children are likely to be confused, not whether adults are. If the goods or services are marketed to sophisticated adults, then the relevant question is whether sophisticated adults are likely to be confused, not whether children or unsophisticated adults are.

The confusion must be shown to be likely to affect a substantial number of people, not just a few. The proper focus is on the "reasonably prudent consumer," not idiosyncratic or unreasonable outliers.

In USPTO proceedings, doubts about likelihood of confusion usually are resolved against the person who is applying for registration of a mark.

SIMILARITY

Marks may be confusingly similar even if they are not identical. Nonidentical marks may be confusingly similar if they look or sound like each other, or have the same or similar meanings, or create similar overall commercial impressions. At bottom, a mark is similar to another mark, for trademark purposes, if, when used in connection with the same or related goods or services, a substantial number of consumers would mistakenly believe the goods or services are from the same source.

Likelihood of confusion does not require proof that confusion is certain to occur, nor even proof that a particular person or group of persons has, in fact, actually become confused. On the other hand, a purely theoretical possibility of confusion will not suffice. Although there is no bright-line test for similarity, the USPTO has developed guidelines. Largely derived from common law, these help trademark examiners make decisions about whether two marks are so similar as to be likely to cause confusion when used in connection with the same or related goods. They are set out in the *Trademark Manual of Examining Procedure* (TMEP). Here are some examples:

Unitary Consideration

When assessing likelihood of confusion, individual parts of a mark are not considered in isolation. Rather, courts assess the similarity of the entire mark, taken as a whole. For example, even though the word *mars* is wholly contained within the word *marsupial*, it is not very likely that consumers would mistake MARS brand products with MARSUPIAL brand products.

This does not mean that individual parts cannot be evaluated separately. An examiner or a court might properly find that BUDWEISER PRIME is confusingly similar to BUDWEISER on the basis of the extreme similarity between the first word of the new mark and the preexisting mark, provided the effect of the addition of the word *prime* on the likelihood of confusion is considered before a final determination is made.

Dominant vs. Peripheral Parts

If the dominant portion of two marks is the same, then the marks may be confusingly similar despite peripheral differences, such as the addition or deletion of word(s) or character(s). For example, MARK LEESML and ML have been deemed confusingly similar when used on the same or closely related goods or services.

Additions or deletions to marks might suffice to avoid likelihood of confusion if (a) the marks in their entireties convey different commercial impressions, or (b) the matter common to the marks is merely descriptive or diluted.

Word Marks

Word marks are evaluated for similarity on the basis of appearance, sound, meaning, and commercial impression. Similarity in one of these respects does not automatically result in a finding of likelihood of confusion even if the goods or services are identical. It may be sufficient to support such a finding, but courts and examiners consider all factors.

Marks that look alike are usually likely to confuse if used with the same or similar goods or services. Homonyms are a good example. The argument that a word has more than one meaning is not extremely persuasive when the same word is used by a competitor as a mark for the same or a similar kind of product. PRUNE COMPUTING, as a mark for computer sales, is likely to be considered confusingly similar to PRUNE COMPUTING as a mark for computer peripherals even though the first claimant may have meant it to refer to a dried plum and the second claimant meant it to connote the act of removing leaves from a plant.

Conversely, marks that look alike are not likely to confuse if used on different goods or services. The more different the goods or services are, the less likely a second use of the same mark is to confuse consumers. A store selling computers under the name APPLE STORE is not likely to be confused with a market selling produce under the same name. Famous or well-known marks are sometimes an exception to this rule, though. (See below.)

Transpositions

Similarity of appearance is sometimes curable by simply changing the order of words, but only if it changes the overall commercial impression. THE WINE SOCIETY OF AMERICA and AMERICAN WINE SOCIETY are likely to cause confusion. BEST JEWELRY and JEWELERS' BEST, on the other hand, is a transposition the TTAB has found to create different commercial impressions.

HOMOPHONES AND MISSPELLINGS

Homophones (words that sound alike) are usually confusingly similar even if they are spelled differently and have different meanings. The words do not have to sound exactly alike. CUP-A-COLA would probably create confusion with COCA-COLA.

A misspelled version of a word is usually confusingly similar to the correctly spelled version. For example, LITE and LIGHT are usually considered confusingly similar.

The USPTO takes the position that there is no correct pronunciation of a mark. Accordingly, the fact that a mark does not sound exactly like another one when it is pronounced correctly will not necessarily prevent a finding of likelihood of confusion, at least if the two possible pronunciations sound very similar. For example, XCEED was denied registration because it sounded too much like X-SEED, even though an argument could be made that they should be pronounced differently. Likewise, SEYCOS and SEIKO were found to be confusingly similar. Changing the spelling or wording of a mark will not necessarily prevent a finding of likelihood of confusion even if the change also alters the sound.

SIMILAR MEANINGS

Synonyms are often found to be confusingly similar. GAS CITY, for example, has been found to be confusingly similar to GAS TOWN. The average consumer is believed to retain only a general impression of a trademark.

For purposes of comparing meanings, the relevant meaning of a word is the one relating to the goods or services in connection with which the mark is used. PLAYERS, used in connection with shoes, connotes playing sports. The same word used in connection with men's underwear would have a different connotation. PLAYERS as a mark for shoes can coexist with PLAYERS as a mark for men's underwear without confusing consumers.

FOREIGN WORDS

The doctrine of foreign equivalents holds that a mark in a foreign language must be translated into English to assess its distinctiveness or its likelihood of confusion with another mark. When applied in the course of assessing likelihood of confusion, however, the doctrine is limited to only those words that an ordinary American purchaser would stop and translate. For this reason, it only applies to common languages; it does not apply to dead or obscure languages. To the extent Latin is a dead language, the doctrine does not apply to it. The doctrine does apply, however, to Latin terms that are still in use today.

The USPTO normally does not apply the doctrine when both marks are in foreign languages. The average American purchaser may be proficient in one foreign language, but is not likely to be proficient in two. The doctrine might be applied, though, if the words are similar, which often happens when the two languages are similar, such as Spanish and Italian.

The USPTO also does not normally apply the doctrine if a foreign phrase has taken on a meaning for Americans that is different from its literal English translation. For example, according to English dictionaries, *cordon bleu* means a skilled chef. The literal translation from French to English, though, would be "blue ribbon." The USPTO would not find BLUE RIBBON similar to CORDON BLEU because in this case the foreign phrase has taken on a whole new meaning to Americans. They are not likely to stop and translate it into English.

Similarity of marks is just one factor to be considered when determining whether two marks are confusingly similar. The fact that a foreign language mark means exactly the same thing as a preexisting mark when translated into English only shows that they are similar in meaning. All other factors (similarity of appearance, sound or commercial impression; relatedness of goods or services; etc.) must be considered.

Doctrine of Legal Equivalents

Under the doctrine of legal equivalents, a word and a visual depiction of it may be considered to be similar in meaning. Thus, a silhouette of a lion's head may be confusingly similar to the word LION. The overall commercial impression must still be considered, however. A visual depiction that is so highly stylized or abstract that it is not likely to cause an association with the word mark might not be deemed confusingly similar.

Families of Marks

When a mark owner employs a common root element in a family of marks, consumers may come to associate the root element with other goods or services on which the mark owner uses it, so that if a new brand name using the same root element appears on the market, the consumer is likely to assume it comes from the same source. The "Mc" in McDONALD'S is an example.

Fonts and Colors ("Stylized Marks")

Generally, the more distinctive the other aspects of a design are, the less important color and font become; and the less distinctive the other aspects of a design are, the more important color or font become. This is why a depiction of a dog peering into a phonograph is likely to be confused with the RCA Victor logo regardless of the colors used, but a depiction of a blue cross is not likely to be confused with the Red

Cross logo. A cross, by itself, is not distinctive. It's the red color that causes people to associate it with the Red Cross organization. A dog peering into a phonograph, in any color, is much more distinctive than a cross.

SURNAMES

Surnames are not trademarks unless they have acquired secondary meaning. A name that is also a word, however, is not considered a surname. It is capable of being inherently distinctive in appropriate circumstances. If, for example, Johnny Bench used BENCH as a trademark for catering services, a court could find that it is inherently distinctive.

When the secondary meaning of a surname is an issue, the test is how it is perceived by prospective customers: Are they likely to associate the surname with the person or with the goods/services?

Famous historical surnames, such as Da Vinci, are not considered surnames for purposes of trademark law. They may be registered without proof of secondary meaning.

A surname combined with generic terms is treated as primarily a surname. A surname combined with a non-generic term is not.

If a surname can be shown to have acquired secondary meaning, trademark remedies may be employed to enforce rights in it. This can impose an unfair burden on those individuals who happen to have been born with the same surname. For example, since JOHNSON'S NURSERY is already federally registered to a man in Wisconsin, theoretically no other person named Johnson may operate a nursery under his own name in the United States. In these kinds of cases, a court may issue a conditional injunction, allowing some limited use of the same name by others, subject to conditions designed to prevent confusion, such as requiring the competitor to display a disclaimer.

Non-trademark use of a personal name, such as the use of one's own name in a mailing address, is not infringement.

Design Marks

Consumers are assumed to retain only general memories of design marks. Accordingly, marks may be confusingly similar even though there are differences between them.

Composite Marks

Composite marks are marks that contain two or more kinds of elements, such as a design with characters. Trademark protection exists only for those elements of a composite mark that could qualify for trademark protection if they stood alone. For example, because the word *bread* in WONDER BREAD is a generic term, it receives no trademark protection when it stands alone. *Wonder* is not generic, so it could receive trademark protection.

For purposes of assessing likelihood of confusion, a mark must be considered as a whole, with greater weight being given to the dominant feature. A word element is often considered dominant because people are most likely to use the wording contained in a mark to refer to the product or service. Nevertheless, there is no general rule about whether words or designs dominate in composite marks; nor is the dominance of a particular element necessarily dispositive.

Parody Marks

Parody marks generally are not likely to cause confusion because the effect of the parody, in most cases, is to create a distinction in the viewer's mind between the actual product or mark, and the joke. This is why LARDASHE is not confusingly similar to JORDACHE. On the other hand, there have been cases where the TTAB has found a parody mark to be likely to confuse. For example, CRACKBERRY was found to be confusingly similar to BLACKBERRY; and LESSBUCKS was found to be confusingly similar to STARBUCKS. The right to use words for the purpose of parody does not necessarily extend to the right to use them as trademarks.

Initial Interest Confusion

A website that attracts visitors by using another firm's trademark (or a very similar one) as its domain name is exploiting what is known as *initial interest confusion*. Some courts hold that initial interest confusion may be sufficient to establish likelihood of confusion even if the consumer is apprised of the true source of the goods upon arrival at the site and before a sale is consummated. To these courts, the use of the mark to lure visitors to the site is infringement even if the homepage of the website disclaims ownership or affiliation with the trademark appearing in its domain name. Not all courts agree.

Relatedness of the Goods or Services

In general, the more similar the goods or services are, the less similar the marks need to be to generate confusion; and the less similar the goods or services are, the more similar the marks have to be to generate confusion. The converse is also true: The more similar the marks are, the less similar the good or services have to be to establish likelihood of confusion; and the less similar the marks are, the more similar the goods will need to be to establish likelihood of confusion.

Using the same or a similar mark on a different but related kind of goods or services can also generate confusion in some cases. This can happen even when the related goods or services are not directly competing. For example, computer peripherals do not compete with computers in the market. People are no less likely to buy a peripheral just because they've already bought a computer, nor are they less likely to buy a computer just because they already have a peripheral. To the contrary, a person who already has a computer is probably more likely to buy a peripheral than she would be if she did not own one. Nevertheless, because the two kinds of goods are related, a consumer could mistakenly believe that both kinds of products emanate from the same source.

A mark that is the same as or similar to an existing trademark generally does not acquire protection as a trademark if the goods or services for which the mark is used are the same as, similar to, or related to the goods or services in connection with which the existing mark is being used. By the same token, an identical or similar mark is not disqualified from trademark protection on the basis of likelihood of confusion if it is used in connection with goods or services that are unrelated to the goods or services that are being marketing under the other trademark. (An exception exists for famous or well-known marks.)

The reason trademark protection is extended not just to goods or services of the same kind but also to different but related goods and services is that consumers generally expect businesses to expand into related areas. Consequently, using the same mark on related goods can create consumer confusion about the source of the goods or services.

USPTO Classifications

The international classification (IC) system the USPTO has created for the processing of trademark registration applications does not determine the relatedness of goods. The fact that two kinds of goods or services are in different IC classes does not necessarily mean they are unrelated, and the fact that two kinds of goods or services are in the same International Class does not necessarily mean they are related in the trademark sense. Umbrellas and whips are both in International Class 18, but a consumer who sees a whip for sale in an adult fantasy shop is not likely to assume it comes from the same company that makes and sells umbrellas.

Indicia of Relatedness

Although there is no bright-line test for relatedness, a few general principles can be gleaned from the cases. For example, consumers may be likely to assume a business is expanding its marketing or sponsorship into a new area if the goods are commonly used together, such as computers and peripherals, or pancake mix and syrup.

Sometimes the fact that two kinds of goods are commonly sold in the same kind of store (e.g., video games and video game consoles) has persuaded a court that the goods are related.

The fact that goods are made from the same kinds of materials and use the same technology might be evidence of relatedness in some cases.

Being marketed through the same channels of trade and advertised through the same media can sometimes help establish relatedness.

Goods or services that are commonly the subject of a license, endorsement or sponsorship may sometimes lead to a finding of relatedness. For example, using the mark used by a fashion magazine on a line of clothing could suggest to consumers that the fashion magazine is related to the clothing in the sense that the magazine endorses, sponsors or licenses the use of its name to the clothing distributor.

Promotional goods are almost always considered related goods because consumers generally assume that trademark owners license their marks to promotional goods manufacturers. A consumer who sees the Disney logo imprinted on pens and ashtrays is likely to assume the Disney Company has licensed the use of its logo to the pencil and ashtray manufacturers.

THE EFFECT OF CONSENT

A prior registrant's consent or waiver of objections to another person's registration of a confusingly similar mark is not binding on the USPTO. Trademark law is also intended to protect consumers from confusion as to source. The existence of a consent agreement is just one factor to be considered in determining likelihood of confusion. It is not controlling.

An agreement that details the particular reasons why the parties believe no likelihood of confusion exists and describes the arrangements the parties have made to avoid confusing the public (such as restricting each other's market), is given considerable weight. Sometimes, though, even a "naked" consent (one that simply sets out the prior registrant's consent to registration without detailing why there's little likelihood of confusion) will be given weight, so long as other factors do not compel a finding of likelihood of confusion.

Collateral Consequences of Confusion

Greater care must be taken to avoid confusion in the case of medical and pharmaceutical products and services because mistakes in the selection and use of these kinds of goods can result in serious and harmful consequences. As a result, a lesser degree of proof is needed to establish likelihood of confusion in these kinds of cases.

Case-by-Case Determination

The rules of thumb set out above are merely guidelines. There is no per se rule in the area of likelihood of confusion. The USPTO and courts consider all relevant facts.

Famous Marks

An exception to the relatedness requirement exists for famous and well-known marks. Using a famous or well-known mark, whether it is a registered or an unregistered one, may result in liability if it is likely to cause confusion, and this is true whether the mark is used on identical, similar, related, or different goods or services. McDonald's, for example, was able to successfully oppose another firm's registration of McBABY for baby furniture even though furniture is not related to food. This is because the "Mc-" format is widely understood to signify products originating from the McDonald's Corporation. McDonald's Corporation has been quite successful in preventing other companies from marketing goods or services this way. In addition to McBABY, it has blocked McSWEET pickled vegetables, a McSLEEP motel chain, and McCLAIM legal services.

Duration

A trademark exists as long as it continues to function as one. Federal registrations are for renewable ten-year terms. Failure to renew a registration results in loss of the benefits of registration, but not necessarily loss of common law trademark rights.

Abandonment

If the owner stops using a mark as a trademark and has no intention of resuming use, the mark is deemed abandoned. Once a mark is abandoned, the exclusive right to use it terminates. A person may become the owner of an abandoned mark by being the first one to use it as a trademark after it is abandoned.

Three continuous years of nonuse gives rise to a presumption of abandonment. The presumption may be rebutted by proof of even minor use during that time, or proof of a plan to resume use.

It is important to distinguish between abandonment of a trademark and abandonment of a trademark registration. A person may abandon a registration in several ways, such as by failing to pursue registration to completion, or failing to timely file a renewal. These things may deprive the owner of the benefits of federal registration, but abandoning a registration does not have the effect of divesting a person or business of ownership of a common law trademark.

Genericide

Another way a mark can cease to function as a trademark is by losing its distinctiveness. This can happen, for example, when a brand name becomes a generic word for a category of products rather than a source identifier.

Infringement

Trademark infringement occurs when a trademark (or something confusingly similar to it) is used in commerce in a way that is likely to cause consumers to be confused about the source, sponsorship or endorsement of particular goods or services. The three possible legal bases for a trademark infringement claim are:

- Section 32 of the Lanham Act[22]
- Section 43(a) of the Lanham Act[23]
- State common law.

A Section 32 claim may be filed only if the mark is federally registered. Section 43(a) and state law claims may be filed whether the mark is federally registered or not. State and federal courts have concurrent jurisdiction to hear Lanham Act claims, but a claim may be brought under the Lanham Act only if the mark is used in interstate or foreign commerce.

Section 32

Section 32 of the Lanham Act is the specific federal prohibition against trademark infringement. To prevail under Section 32, a claimant must prove:

(a) a federally registered mark
(b) a copy, counterfeit or imitation of which
(c) is used in interstate or foreign commerce
(d) in connection with a sale, offer, distribution, or advertising
(e) without the trademark owner's consent
(f) in a way that is likely to cause confusion or deceive consumers.

---

22 15 U.S.C. § 1114 (2017).

23 15 U.S.C. § 1125(a) (2017).

Of course, to establish the first element, it is necessary to prove that a valid trademark exists, which means that the distinctiveness requirement must be satisfied. Federal registration gives rise to a presumption that the trademark is valid, though.

Section 43(a)

Section 43(a) of the Lanham Act prohibits unfair competition by means of false or misleading labeling, packaging or advertising. It is broad enough that it can be used as another avenue of recourse for trademark infringement claims, such as when not all of the requirements for a Section 32 claim are satisfied. For example, it may be used to seek redress for the infringement of a trademark that is not federally registered. This does not mean that Section 43(a) is exclusively for common law trademark infringement claims. In many cases, a claim for infringement of a registered trademark may be brought under either Section 32 or Section 43(a), or both.

To prevail on a claim under Section 43(a), a claimant must prove:

(a) a word, name, symbol, device, trade dress, or combination thereof, or a false designation of origin, or a false or misleading statement of fact

(b) is used in interstate or foreign commerce

(c) in connection with goods or services, or containers for them

(d) in a way that either is likely to cause confusion or deceive as to the origin, sponsorship or endorsement of the goods or services, or likely to confuse or deceive as to a person's affiliation, connection or association with another person, or misrepresents the nature, qualities or geographic origin of goods or services, in advertising.

In cases where Section 43(a) standing is predicated on infringement of a competitor's trade dress, a further showing must be made that the trade dress is nonfunctional.

A Section 43(a) claim may be brought by any person who believes she is likely to be damaged by the false or misleading material. This could include a person who believes the material infringes her trademark because it involves the use of a word or device that is likely to cause confusion or deceive as to the origin, sponsorship or endorsement of goods or services. Unlike Section 32 and state claims, however, likelihood of confusion about the origin of the goods need not be proven if it can be shown that the mark was used in a way that misrepresents the nature or qualities of goods or services.

Infringement can occur in many ways. Explicitly marketing a product or service using a mark that is confusingly similar to another is one way, but implicitly associating another's mark with a different product or service can also result in liability. Positioning a photograph of the Rolex logo in close proximity to other kinds of watches that are offered for sale on a website is an example. Visitors to the site would be likely to mistakenly believe the watches being offered are Rolex watches. Similarly, a photograph of the Ford Motor Company logo on an auto repair service's website might cause visitors to the site to mistakenly believe the repair service is sponsored or endorsed by Ford. Trademark infringement liability may arise in these kinds of scenarios because the "likelihood of confusion" standard is governed not by what a logician would infer, but by what an average consumer would infer.

State law claims

A state infringement claim may be brought to enforce rights in a mark whether or not it is registered with the USPTO, and whether or not it is used in interstate or foreign commerce.

To prevail on a common law trademark infringement claim, the claimant must prove:

(a) ownership of a valid trademark
(b) another person's use of the same or a similar mark as a trademark; and

(c) likelihood of confusion as to origin, sponsorship, endorsement, association or affiliation.

Infringement is a **strict liability** tort. Neither intent nor bad faith need be proven in order to prevail on a claim of infringement. Both malicious and innocent infringement are unlawful.

Palming off

Palming off (or "passing off") occurs when a person infringes a trademark in bad faith, or with intent to deceive consumers about the source of goods or services, by using another person's trademark to market goods from a different source. Putting *Chips Ahoy!* brand cookies in Pepperidge Farm packages or sewing Gucci labels on clothing purchased from Goodwill are examples.

A cause of action for palming off arises at common law and under Section 43(a) when a seller misleads customers into believing that the goods he is selling are a competitor's when they really are not. A seller might be tempted to do this, for example, if his own wares are inferior or if the seller has not yet developed a strong reputation.

Reverse palming off

Some states also recognize a cause of action for reverse palming off. This occurs when a company removes another company's trademark from a product before reselling it. Instead of luring customers into a sale by making them believe it was made by someone else, reverse palming off involves concealing the original source of a product.

Counterfeiting

Counterfeiting is specific kind of infringement in which an identical mark is used on the same or similar goods from a different source by someone without trademark rights.

A counterfeiting claim brought pursuant to the Lanham Act requires proof that the mark is identical to a federally registered mark.

In addition to being actionable as infringement, counterfeiting is a crime.

Contributory infringement

In some cases, a person may be held liable for infringement even if she was not the one who actually performed the infringing act, if she facilitated or contributed in some way to the infringing act. Specifically, a person may be liable for contributory infringement if she does one of the following:

- intentionally induces another person to infringe a trademark;
- continues to supply products to a person whom she knows or has reason to know is mislabeling them; or
- provides a service (such as a website) or some other mechanism over which she has control that enables the infringing activity, with knowledge or reason to know that the infringing activity is occurring there, and fails to stop the infringement from occurring (such as by disabling or suspending the infringer's account).

A lessor or swap meet manager who rents space to a vendor whom he knows is engaging in infringing activity on the premises, but does nothing to stop it, could incur contributory liability for infringement. In the same way, a web hosting service or website operator who knows or has reason to know of third-party content infringing a trademark but fails to remove it may incur contributory liability for the infringement.

Knowledge is generally a necessary element of a contributory infringement claim. A person may be held liable for contributory infringement only if he knew or should have known that infringing activity was occurring. Generalized awareness of a theoretical possibility of infringing uses is not enough. On the other hand, courts do not countenance willful blindness, i.e., deliberately avoiding learning of actual instances of infringement. In short, to prevail on a contributory liability claim, the plaintiff must demonstrate either of two things about the defendant:

- actual knowledge; or
- willful blindness.

Willful blindness means a deliberate failure to investigate, despite having reason to suspect infringement.

Liability may attach if in addition to providing the instrumentality or mechanism, the provider actively encourages, solicits or induces infringing uses, or has knowledge or reason to know of specific instances of actual infringement and deliberately fails to either investigate or take action to stop the infringing activity.

Only a person who has direct control over the content of a website may be held contributorily liable for it. *Direct control* means the ability and power to allow or remove content from a site.

Vicarious infringement

A principal may be vicariously liable for the infringing acts of an agent. An employer may be vicariously liable for the infringing acts of an employee within the course and scope of the employment. Partners may be vicariously liable for the infringing acts of other partners.

Dilution

Dilution means the unauthorized use of a famous mark in a way that tarnishes it or weakens its distinctiveness. It is an entirely statutory cause of action, originating in Section 43(c)[24] of the Lanham Act and analogous state statutes.

---

[24] 15 U.S.C. § 1125(c) (2017).

The elements of a Section 43(c) dilution claim are:

(a) commercial use in interstate commerce
(b) of a famous and distinctive mark, or a mark that is so similar to the famous mark that it gives rise to an association between the marks
(c) beginning after the mark became famous
(d) causing, or likely to cause, blurring or tarnishment, that is, loss of distinctiveness or reputational harm.

The use does not need to be on related or competing goods, and it does not have to be likely to cause confusion. No proof of economic loss is required. The purpose of the dilution cause of action is not to protect the public from confusion about the source, sponsorship or endorsement of goods and services. Rather, it is to protect a company's investment in its trademark. Federal registration is not a precondition to asserting a dilution claim.

The elements of a state cause of action for dilution are usually:

(a) a strong (distinctive) mark; and
(b) likelihood of dilution.

A few states only require a showing of distinctiveness. The majority rule, however, is that the mark must also be famous. The line between distinctiveness and fame is not always clear. According to the Restatement (3d) of Unfair Competition, the relevant test, for common law trademark dilution purposes, is whether a mark evokes, in the public's mind, an association with a specific source only when used in connection with particular goods or service. If it does, then it is not sufficiently distinctive to be protectable against dilution. This standard approximates the "fame" requirement in the federal statute.

Fame

Fame is a required element of a federal dilution claim. The mark must be sufficiently well-known that it retains its significance as a source indicator even outside the context of the goods or services with which it is used. If consumers only associate it with those goods or services, then it is not strong enough to merit federal protection from dilution. This means that only famous or well-known marks qualify for federal legal protection against dilution. The vast majority of marks do not.

Factors federal courts consider when determining the fame of a mark include:

- the degree of inherent or acquired distinctiveness
- how widely the mark has been used by its owner
- how long mark has been used
- the duration and extent of advertising and publicity of the mark
- the scope of the geographic area in which the mark has been used
- the channels of trade in which the goods or services are marketed
- the degree of recognition of the mark in the trading areas and the channels of trade used by the trademark owner and the alleged diluter
- the nature and extent of the use of same or similar marks by third parties
- whether the mark is federally registered.

Registration is not required in order to file or prevail on a federal trademark dilution claim.

Blurring

Blurring means lessening the strength (distinctiveness) of a mark as an identifier of source, reducing its capacity to distinguish and identify goods and services as coming from one source rather than another. An example would be selling tennis shoes under the ROLEX name. Because people associate that brand name with watches, the likelihood that they would mistakenly believe the shoes are coming from the same source as ROLEX watches may not be great. Nevertheless, the company that makes ROLEX watches has an interest in preserving the public's association of that name with high quality watches, and not with just any product or service. Using it in this way makes it less clear that goods marketed under the ROLEX name originate from the high-quality watchmaking company.

Tarnishment

Tarnishment means causing a mark to have a negative association in the public's mind. This may occur as a result of the unauthorized use of another person's mark on inferior quality or hazardous goods, or in an unwholesome or unsavory context.

At first glance, tarnishment law would seem to provide a way for businesses to shut down criticism and bad reviews. Trademark law, however, attempts to promote First Amendment values by shielding those who mention or display a trademark in criticism, commentary, opinion, or parody from trademark liability. Referring to a trademark strictly for these purposes is fair use, so long as the content is not false or misleading.

Remedies

The two basic legal remedies for a victim of trademark infringement are money damages and injunctive relief. In counterfeiting cases, the claimant may elect either treble damages or statutory damages. Willful infringement may also be punishable criminally.

Damages for dilution may be recovered only if intent to cause dilution or to trade on the reputation of the famous mark is proven. In all other cases, relief is limited to an injunction.

Compensatory damages compensate the trademark owner for decreased sales as a result of consumer confusion, losses incurred as a result of having to sell at a discount in order to compete with the infringer, and the cost of corrective advertising and other expenses incurred in attempting to clear up the confusion the infringement caused. They also compensate the trademark owner for harm to reputation and diminution of good will. A trademark owner may also seek compensation for the loss of a reasonable royalty that would have accrued from licensing the mark to the defendant.

If an infringer acts willfully or in bad faith (i.e., intended to cause confusion or deception), or engaged in palming off, then a court may order him to turn over the profits he has made by virtue of the infringing use. An innocent infringer is not required to forfeit profits made as a result of the infringing use.

Treble damages may be awarded if the infringement was willful. Intent to infringe is not enough, however. Treble damages will be awarded only if the infringer acted with knowledge that its conduct was unlawful, or if the infringer was recklessly indifferent to the law. Punitive damages are rarely awarded, but are possible if an infringer's conduct is particularly egregious.

In exceptional cases, a court may order the infringer to pay the trademark owner's attorney fees. This might be ordered, for example, in cases where the infringement was willful, deliberate, fraudulent or malicious, or when it involves counterfeiting. Conversely, if the trademark owner filed the case in bad faith, or the court determines the claim is frivolous (i.e., has no reasonable basis in law or fact), then it may order the trademark owner to pay the defendant's attorney fees.

An injunction may be issued if the remedy at law (i.e., money damages) is not adequate. Injunctive relief is usually appropriate in trademark infringement cases because infringement is a continuing wrong, so money damages alone normally are not adequate. An infringer's voluntary suspension of infringing activities will not prevent a court from issuing an injunction.

When a court grants injunctive relief, it may do more than simply prohibit use of the mark. It may also order other things, either in addition to that or as alternatives to it. For example, a court might order the infringer to destroy or turn over infringing labels, packaging, and advertisements; or to display a disclaimer; or to notify distributors that it is not affiliated with the trademark owner; or to publish corrective advertising; or to recall products bearing infringing labels.

In counterfeiting cases, the trademark owner may ask the court to issue an ex parte seizure order. *Ex parte* means it may be issued without advance notice to the alleged infringer. The person seeking the order must post financial security (usually a bond), notify the United States Attorney, and make the showings necessary for ex parte equitable relief (irreparable harm; likelihood of success on the merits, and so on). The claimant must not publicize the seizure request prior to making it; must show that the alleged infringer is likely to move, hide or destroy the goods if he receives notice of the application for a seizure order; and must provide the court with the location of the items to be seized. A hearing must be held promptly after the ex parte order is issued. A defendant may sue for any damages caused by a wrongful seizure.

Seizure of infringing imports

An aggrieved trademark owner may also ask the U.S. Customs Service to seize counterfeit goods or goods bearing a mark that is confusingly similar to a registered mark. To pursue this course of action, the trademark owner must record the registered mark with the U.S. Customs Service. The Customs Service may, but is not required to, seize goods bearing counterfeit marks that are not federally registered.

Criminal penalties

Intentional or attempted trafficking in goods or services using a counterfeit trademark(s) with knowledge that the mark is counterfeit is a felony crime under the Trademark Counterfeiting Act. It is punishable by up to ten years and a $2,000,000 fine for a first offense; and up to twenty years and a $5,000,000 fine for a subsequent offense.

Many states also have laws making trademark counterfeiting a crime.

Trademark counterfeiting is a predicate act for RICO purposes.

Defenses

General denial

The first sale doctrine

Trademark rights are exhausted in the first sale. This means that after a consumer buys a product with a trademark affixed to it, he can resell the item with or without the trademark affixed to it. For example, if Mary goes to the store and buys a Hasbro® game, she can freely resell the game, even inside the box with the Hasbro label on it, at her garage sale.

To qualify for this defense, the subsequent sale must be conducted in a truthful fashion, and in a way that is not likely to confuse the public as to the source of the goods. The first sale doctrine is not available as a defense for a person who buys products from one company and then tries to resell them with another company's label attached to them. For the defense to apply, the goods must be genuine.

Resales must comply with the trademark owner's quality control requirements.

Resale of repackaged goods is also permitted, but only if the fact of repackaging is disclosed; the repackager's name is disclosed; a disclaimer of the repackager's association with the trademark owner is displayed; and no "undue prominence" is given to the trademark. Also, the repackaging must not lower the quality of the goods. If it does, then the trademark owner may sue the repackager for trademark dilution.

The general rule is that the goods will not qualify for the First Sale defense if they have been modified prior to the resale. In some circumstances, though, resale of repaired or reconditioned goods may qualify for the protection of the First Sale doctrine. If the fact that the goods are used is disclosed, any material information about the repair is disclosed, and the repair or reconditioning is not so extensive that the product cannot really be considered the same anymore, then the product may be resold, with or without the original trademark affixed.

A resale of a product that has the effect of voiding a warranty is considered a modification of the product. The first sale doctrine cannot be asserted as a defense with respect to these kinds of sales.

Because of the truthfulness requirement, a reseller who falsely states or implies that she is an authorized reseller, or that she has some other relationship with the trademark owner that really does not exist, would not be protected by the first sale doctrine.

Finally, the First Sale defense is not available to a reseller of gray market goods. *Gray market goods* are goods that are imported into the United States bearing a trademark that is confusingly similar to a U.S. trademark, without the consent of the owner of the U.S. trademark. The first sale doctrine cannot be asserted as a defense in this situation because the imported goods are not considered genuine. Even if the trademark affixed to the imported goods was properly registered and legally placed on the goods in the country of origin, the appearance of the mark on the goods in the United States identifies them as originating from the owner of the federally registered mark (the U.S. owner). Since they did not really originate from the U.S. owner, the goods are not genuine. Accordingly, the first sale doctrine will not be available as a defense. An exception exists when the foreign and domestic trademark owner is the same person or there is common control between the foreign and domestic trademark owners (such as where the foreign trademark owner is a parent or subsidiary corporation of the U.S. trademark owner) and the foreign goods are identical to the domestic goods. If they are not identical, then the foreign goods must bear a label giving notice to consumers that they are not physically identical to the

American-made goods. Under Customs Service regulations, the notice must be essentially as follows: "This product is not a product authorized by the U.S. trademark owner for importation and is physically and materially different from the authorized product."

Fair use

Nominative Fair Use

Merely referring to a trademark (as distinguished from using it in a way that suggests something untrue about the origin, sponsorship or endorsement of goods or services) is not infringement. Using a trademark this way is called *nominative fair use.* It is also sometimes called "referential" or "trademark fair use." It is a defense to both infringement and dilution claims.

The referential use must be both truthful and not likely to confuse the public about the source, sponsorship or endorsement of products or services. Thus, a repair service may refer to the brand names of products it repairs or services so long as it does not falsely state or imply that it is authorized by or affiliated with the owner of the trademark in some way. Likewise, a shop may sell brand name replacement parts so long as it does not falsely hold itself out as an "authorized" seller or an "affiliate" of the trademark owner.

Courts impose three conditions on this defense:

1) The product or service is not readily identifiable without using the trademark;
2) Only so much of the mark is used as is reasonably necessary to identify the product or service;
3) The user does not state or imply sponsorship or endorsement by the trademark owner.

The defense is commonly associated with the right to use trademarks in reporting, commentary, criticism, parody, and comparative advertising, but it can also apply in other contexts, too.

Referential use of a mark is also permitted if the trademarked product is a component part of another product or service, so long as the public would not be led to believe that the trademark owner is either the source or sponsor of the other product or service. This is sometimes called *collateral use.* An auto parts dealer selling "reconditioned Ford parts" would be an example (so long as no claim is made or implied that the parts are authorized or approved by Ford).

Comparative Advertising

A truthful reference to a competitor's brand name in comparative advertising is fair use. It is not actionable as dilution, either. The Lanham Act expressly provides that there will be no liability for dilution when a famous mark is used in comparative advertising, provided the mark is not altered or parodied.

The right to engage in comparative advertising does not include a right to make false or misleading statements.

Descriptive Fair Use

Descriptive use is another kind of fair use defense that is available in trademark infringement and dilution cases. Sellers are allowed to use ordinary words to describe their own goods or services even if those words happen to be part of someone else's trademark. For example, if the owner of the trademark, SWEETARTS, which is a telescoped composite of the words *sweet* and *tart*, were to sue a company for infringement for advertising its product as "sweet and tart," the company could assert the defense of descriptive fair use on the basis that it is merely using ordinary words that accurately describe its product or service. Similarly, a new car dealer who happens to have a sales location in Lincoln, Nebraska could advertise its "Lincoln store" even though someone else owns LINCOLN as a registered mark for sales of Lincoln automobiles.

Using one's own personal name in connection with a business is another example of descriptive fair use. If Samuel Adams decides to go into business using his own name as the name of his business, he could assert the Descriptive Fair Use defense if the beer maker were to sue him for infringement.

The defense is lost if the descriptive term is used as a trademark. A firm advertising "sweet and juicy oranges" could probably prevail using the Descriptive Fair Use defense if sued by the owner of the trademark SWEET 'N JUICY. If, however, it was to start using "Sweet and Juicy" as a brand name for the oranges (in other words, as an identifier of the source of the oranges, such as by using that phrase on labels), then it would lose the protection of the Descriptive Fair Use defense.

Also, the defense is available only if the descriptive use is truthful and used in good faith. Using a mark with the intention of confusing consumers about the source of the goods or services, or with the intention of exploiting an existing trademark's reputation, exemplifies bad faith.

NONCOMMERCIAL USE, CRITICISM, COMMENTARY AND PARODY

Criticism, commentary, opinion, and parody are protected by the First Amendment. References to a trademark for these purposes, by persons other than business competitors of the trademark owner, normally are fair use. In fact, any expressive use of a mark for purposes other than competition or commercial exploitation is usually fair use. The Lanham Act prohibits the unauthorized use in commerce of a trademark "in connection with the sale, offering for sale, distribution or advertising of goods and services." State laws vary, but all require a person claiming trademark infringement to prove that the use being made of a mark creates a likelihood of confusion with someone else's goods or services that are being marketed under the same or a similar trademark. For this reason, merely referring to someone else's trademark for a noncommercial purpose is not likely to result in liability for infringement. Trademark infringement liability should be a concern only when someone else's mark or something similar to it is being used to sell, lease, offer or advertise goods or services.

The Lanham Act specifically excludes noncommercial uses of a trademark from the definition of dilution by tarnishment. Accordingly, there should be no need to worry about potential dilution liability for things like an incidental display of trademarks in a photograph of a cityscape, or references to brand names in an unpaid product review.

The likelihood of confusion as to source is a useful guide for deciding whether a use of a mark is a non-expressive, commercial use. The greater the likelihood of confusing consumers about the source of the product, the more likely it is being used for a non-expressive, commercial purpose.

The Lanham Act expressly exempts news reporting, parody, and commentary from dilution liability, but noncommercial use is a defense to a dilution claim only if the mark is not altered. Using an altered mark, even in a parody, may not be a defense against a dilution claim.

Using a mark to truthfully describe one's background or achievements (such as in an advertisement for expert consulting services) is not considered a commercial use, and will not expose a person to liability for dilution.

A website may be "commercial" if it offers a product or service for sale or lease, displays links to commercial web sites, or if there is advertising on it. A paid product review is considered a form of advertising. Nevertheless, even a commercial website is exempt from dilution liability when it uses an unaltered trademark solely for the purpose of criticism, commentary or parody, so long as the content is not false or misleading.

Statute of limitations

There is no specific federal statute of limitations for trademark infringement or dilution claims, so federal courts apply state law to determine the appropriate limitations period.

Laches

Even in the absence of a statute of limitations, courts have inherent authority ("equity power") to deny relief to a claimant whose unreasonable delay in enforcing rights results in prejudice to the alleged violator. This defense is called *laches.*

Unlike a statute of limitations, there is no fixed number of years that must pass in order for the laches defense to apply. Any unreasonable delay in filing a claim may suffice. Unreasonable-ness is decided on a case-by-case basis. Although a court might rely on an analogous state statute of limitations as a guideline, it is not bound by any specific statutory period.

Three things must be established:

- Knowledge of the wrongful use of the mark;
- Delay in bringing a lawsuit; and
- Prejudice.

Prejudice, in this context, means the trademark violator changed his position to his detriment during the period of delay. The best example of prejudice would be an infringer's substantial investment in a business on the basis of an assumption that the claimant had no objection to the infringing use.

Laches may be invoked as a defense against the enforcement of a common law or registered trademark, even "incontestable" ones. It may be asserted as a defense to intentional infringement or dilution only if the delay is so prolonged and inexcusable that it is or comes very close to being an abandonment of trademark rights.

Acquiescence

Acquiescence is an equitable defense that may be asserted when a trademark owner intentionally signals to the violator that the infringing or diluting use is acceptable.

Equitable estoppel

Equitable estoppel is a defense courts devised to bar ("estop") a party to litigation from taking unfair advantage of another by asserting a position in litigation that is inconsistent with one he previously asserted, if the other party detrimentally relied on the previous position. All of the following must be proven in order to prevail on an estoppel defense:

- misrepresentation or concealment of a material fact
- knowledge of the facts at the time of the representation or concealment
- lack of knowledge of those facts on the defendant's part
- intent or expectation that the other party will act on the basis of the representation or concealment
- detrimental reliance on the misrepresentation or concealment.

Unclean hands

A court may use its equity power to deny requested relief to a person who acts with unclean hands, that is, a person who is guilty of misconduct himself, provided the misconduct relates to the claim in some way. The "unclean hands" defense may be asserted even if the mark is registered and "incontestable."

Abandonment

A trademark owner can lose trademark rights through abandonment. This occurs when the trademark owner stops using a mark and has no intention of resuming use in the reasonably foreseeable future.

A sustained period of nonuse can be evidence of intent not to resume use. There is no precise definition of how long a "sustained period of nonuse" is. For registered marks, though, nonuse for three consecutive years creates a presumption of abandonment.

The period of nonuse must be continuous in order for abandonment to be found to have occurred. Intermittent periods of nonuse or diminished use do not count. The presumption of abandonment of a federally registered mark will not be applicable if the claimant makes at least some use of the mark during the three-year period.

Abandonment is not a defense to an infringement claim if the nonuse is due to circumstances that are beyond the owner's control, provided use is resumed when circumstances change.

Token use (e.g., making a couple of sales to friends just to keep trademark protection alive) is treated the same as nonuse.

An owner's abandonment of all use of a mark results in loss of all trademark rights in the mark. If he continues to use the mark on other goods or services covered by the mark, however, then only the right to use the mark in connection with the goods and services as to which he has failed to use the mark will be deemed abandoned.

It is possible for the geographic scope of a common law trademark to shrink over time. This can happen when the owner ceases using the mark in a particular geographic area. The geographic scope of a common law trademark will not include areas in which the mark is no longer being used, if it is shown that the trademark owner has no intention of resuming use in those areas within the reasonably foreseeable future. In other words, a common law trademark can be deemed abandoned in some parts of the geographic region in which the mark had been protected, yet continue to exist in other areas. This is not the case with federally registered marks. Federally registered marks generally enjoy nationwide protection even if they are not used in all regions of the country.

For purposes of the abandonment defense, advertising is not considered use of a trademark.

Naked licensing

A trademark owner has an affirmative obligation to supervise the use of the mark by licensees (if any) to make sure they observe consistent standards of quality. Giving another person permission to use one's trademark in whatever way he sees fit, without retaining any control over his use of the mark, is called *naked licensing*. Naked licensing can result in a finding of abandonment of the mark.

Fraudulent registration

Fraud in procuring or maintaining a trademark registration may be asserted as a defense to an infringement claim, even if the trademark registration has become "incontestable." To establish fraudulent registration, it is necessary to prove each of the following elements:

- false or misleading representation to, or concealment of information from, the USPTO
- the representation or concealment pertains to a material fact
- knowledge of falsity or misleading nature, or reckless disregard for the truth
- intent to deceive.

A fact is material if it can be shown that registration or renewal, as the case may be, would not have been granted but for the false or misleading representation, or that it would have been denied if the USPTO had known concealed information.

Trademark applicants and renewal registrants have a duty of inquiry with respect to certain kinds of material information, such as whether the claimant is using the mark on the kinds of goods or services listed in the application or registration. Failing to ascertain the truth of essential facts like these can amount to "reckless disregard for the truth."

An amendment to correct a materially false or misleading statement of use in an application for registration or renewal of a trademark will not remedy the fraud if the original fraud was intentional.

Fraudulent registration is not only a defense to an infringement claim; it can also be grounds for a tort claim. If a person or business is injured by a fraudulent registration of a trademark, the registrant may be sued for money damages under the Lanham Act.[347]

Proof that a registration or renewal was procured by fraud normally only invalidates the registration; it does not invalidate any underlying common law trademark that may exist. If the fraud is egregious enough, though, it might be possible to assert an "unclean hands" defense against a claim of infringement of the common law mark.

Assignments in gross

An assignment in gross is a transfer of a trademark separate from the goodwill associated with it. Assignments in gross are void and unenforceable.

Goodwill refers to the expectancy of continued patronage based on the benefit and advantage of an established reputation.

The purpose of the rule against assignments in gross is to protect the public from confusion about the source of particular goods or services.

The rule can be easier to state than to apply. Courts attempt to interpret and apply the rule in way that will serve its purpose, namely, to protect consumers by preserving the significance of the mark to them.

Conveying both the mark and the physical assets used to produce the goods or render the service associated with the mark is usually deemed sufficient to transfer goodwill with the mark. Such a conveyance, however, will not suffice if the assignee uses the mark on goods or services that are of a fundamentally different nature.

Conveying physical assets is not the only way to transfer goodwill along with a mark. If the assignee continues to produce goods of the same nature and quality as the ones previously associated with the trademark, then goodwill may be deemed to have been conveyed along with the mark even if no physical assets were transferred.

For a trademark in goods, the conveyance of a needed trade secret, patent or copyright along with the mark might establish a transfer of goodwill.

For service marks, continuity of management sometimes suffices to establish a transfer of goodwill. It may not be possible to make a valid assignment of a service mark for a personal service business that is bound up with the mark owner's personal skill (e.g., a medical doctor.)

Since it is not possible for goodwill to exist a mark has been used, trademark transfers prior to use are invalid assignments in gross. In addition, the Lanham Act specifically prohibits assignments of rights in an intent-to-use registration application prior to use.

Because an assignment in gross is void, nonuse of a mark by the original trademark owner after an assignment in gross may result in a finding of abandonment of the mark on the part of the original trademark owner.

Registration

Benefits of registration

- presumption of validity and ownership of the trademark
- nationwide scope of protection
- deterrence of infringement
- constructive notice of the existence and ownership of the trademark
- right to sue in federal court
- can be used to prevent importation of infringing products
- protection against cybersquatters
- basis for foreign registration

Federal vs. state

Trademarks may be registered with the federal government, a state government, or both. State registration only gives the registrant a presumptive right to use the mark throughout the state, not throughout the country. A federal registration gives the registrant a presumptive right to use it anywhere in the country. Obtaining a federal registration makes it unnecessary to register the mark in each individual state where the mark is used.

Geographic scope

Trademarks are territorial. The owner's exclusive right to use one is limited to the geographic area in which it has been used plus any other geographic area in which people have come to associate it with the owner's goods or services. The geographic area in which a mark is used, together with the geographic regions to which reputation and goodwill have spread, is called the *area of trade.* Federal registration presumptively extends the geographic scope of a trademark to the borders of the entire country.

CONCURRENT USE

Courts have equitable power to allow concurrent use of the same or similar marks in a way that is not likely to cause confusion, such as by limiting the geographic scope of the sales territory of one or both owners. This can be an option where, for example, a business has a federally registered trademark that is the same as or confusingly similar to an unregistered mark and the owner of the unregistered mark is able to prove prior use. In this situation, depending on the circumstances, the USPTO or a court might declare that the common law trademark owner has the exclusive right to use the mark in a specified geographic area, while the owner of the registered mark has the exclusive right to use it everywhere else. Businesses may also stipulate to this kind of arrangement as a way of settling trademark disputes.

To register a mark for a specified geographic area instead of one with nationwide scope, a concurrent use application should be filed.

A concurrent use registration is allowed only if the applicant used the mark prior to the date another party registered it, and then only if registration of both marks is not likely to cause confusion. There must be either a judicial or TTAB determination of concurrent rights to use the same mark. Filing a concurrent use application initiates a TTAB concurrent use proceeding.

Use vs. *Intent to Use*

Trademark applications may be based on either use or intent to use. If an intent-to-use application is filed, then actual use of the mark in commerce must begin within six months (plus any extensions that are granted) after the application is filed. Evidence of use must be submitted during that same time period.

Under the Lanham Act, the filing of an intent-to-use application is constructive use of the mark. This means that if the applicant files sufficient evidence of use within the allotted time, then the date of use will relate back to the date the application was filed. That is to say, the trademark will be treated as if it was first being used on the date the original application was filed. If the applicant does not properly file such evidence during the allotted time, then the application will be rejected and the benefit of the intent-to-use rule is lost.

Principal vs. *Supplemental Registers*

The USPTO offers two kinds of registration. The Principal Register is for marks that currently meet all requirements for registration as a trademark. The Supplemental Register is for things that do not currently meet all requirements for federal registration as a trademark but could potentially qualify in the future.

The most common reason for placement on the Supplemental Register is failure to satisfy the distinctiveness requirement. A mark that is not inherently distinctive would go on the Supplemental Register if it has not yet acquired secondary meaning. Being on the Supplemental Register essentially notifies the world that a mark does not currently qualify for federal trademark protection but someone is working on it. The owner of a mark that is on the Supplemental Register may apply to have it listed on the Principal Register once it has acquired distinctiveness.

A mark that creates a likelihood of confusion with a previously registered mark is not even potentially registrable. Therefore, it may not be included on either the Principal or the Supplemental Register. Because the USPTO may refuse a registration on the basis that it is confusingly similar to a mark on either register, getting a mark on the Supplemental Register can help deter others from trying to register it. This could be important if, for example, a company needs to work on building secondary meaning before a mark will qualify for registration on the Principal Register.

Inclusion on the Supplemental Register does not create a presumption of validity, ownership, or right to use the mark, is not deemed to be constructive notice or use of the mark, and does not give the claimant a right to block importation.

Registration of a mark on either the Supplemental or the Principal Register gives the owner the right to use the ® symbol.

The remainder of this discussion addresses the requirements for inclusion on the Principal Register.

Exclusions from registration

INVALID TRADEMARK

Only a valid trademark may be registered. Before approving an application for registration of a trademark, the USPTO will attempt to determine whether it is confusingly similar to an existing one. Doubts about likelihood of confusion are resolved against the applicant.

In rare cases, the USPTO may allow concurrent use of an identical or similar mark for the same or related goods, subject to conditions and limitations on use to ensure there will be no confusion among consumers as to the source of the goods or services. The USPTO will not do this, however, unless it is convinced that it can be done without confusing consumers.

WHOLLY INTRASTATE COMMERCE

The Commerce Clause of the federal constitution only authorizes Congress to regulate interstate and foreign commerce. Therefore, only those trademarks that are used in interstate or foreign commerce can be federally registered. A wholly intrastate trademark may be registered with a state trademark office and enforced as a common law trademark.

LIVING PERSON'S NAME, SIGNATURE, OR PORTRAIT

The USPTO will not allow the registration of a living person's name, signature or portrait without the person's consent. The rule applies not only to full names, but also surnames, first names, shortened names, nicknames, pseudonyms and titles.

This rule only applies to situations in which the public would recognize and understand the name, signature or portrait as identifying a particular living individual who is likely to be associated with the goods or services, either because the person is publicly connected with the business or industry in which the mark is used, or because the person is so famous or well-known that the public would reasonably assume a connection.

The fact that a name is used by more than one person does not negate the consent requirement if the mark identifies, to the relevant public, a famous person or a person who is publicly connected with the business or industry.

When consent is required, it must be in writing and signed. The writing must specifically give consent to the registration of the name, signature or portrait as a trademark. Merely consenting to the use of the mark will not suffice as consent to registration. Consent is presumed if the person whose name or likeness is used in a mark is the one who signs his name to the application for registration.

The rule against registration of a name without consent does not bar registration of names that only coincidentally happen to be names of real persons. A connection between the person and the business or industry must exist in the public's mind, or the name must be so famous or well-known that the public could interpret its use on a product as indicating that person's connection to or endorsement of the product. The fact that the Tom James Company has registered the mark TOM JAMES in connection with the sale of clothing does not mean that a lawyer named Tom James has the right to have the registration cancelled because he did not consent to it. The public is not likely to associate an attorney with clothing sales.

Dead U.S. President's Name, Signature or Portrait

The name, signature or portrait of a dead U.S. President may not be registered as a trademark if the President's spouse is still living and has not consented to the registration. The surviving spouse's consent is required even if another person has or had the same name as the President. For example, if former president Bill Clinton dies, it will be necessary to obtain Hillary's consent in order to register his name, signature or likeness as a trademark, even though a lot of people are named Bill Clinton. The consent must be in writing and signed.

Flags, Coats of Arms, Insignias, etc.

Flags, coats of arms, insignias, etc. of a governmental unit—whether national, state or municipal—generally cannot be registered as trademarks.

Designations of certain private organizations also may not be registered. Congress has granted exclusive rights to specified organizations to use certain words, symbols and designations. The American Legion, Boy Scouts, Girl Scouts and Little League are examples.

Federally Protected Slogans, Words and Symbols

The federal government prohibits the registration of certain words, slogans and symbols, for reasons usually (but not always) having to do with protecting the government's proprietary interest in intellectual property. The USPTO will deny registration to a mark that employs such a slogan, word or symbol. Smokey Bear, the words *Olympic* and *Copyright*, the Red Cross symbol, and the slogan, "Give a Hoot, Don't Pollute" are examples.

False Association with a Person, Institution, Belief, or National Symbol

Marks falsely suggesting a connection to a person, whether living or dead, are not registrable. Marks falsely suggesting a connection to an institution, belief, or national symbol also are not registrable. The rule does not apply to the use of the name or likeness of a historical figure who has been dead for a long time. Incorporating a drawing of Paul Revere into a company's logo is permissible, for instance.

Geographic Names

The names of countries, states, cities, counties, mountains, rivers, or any other geographic region cannot be registered with the USPTO unless acquired secondary meaning can be shown. The same is true of drawings and maps of them.

This rule is subject to three exceptions:

- Planetary and extraterrestrial terms
- Remote, obscure places
- Uses that are obviously not indicative of geographic source.

These kinds of uses are considered inherently distinctive.

Primarily geographical terms that are deceptively misdescriptive words are not registrable under any circumstances. A geographic misdescription is deceptive if a consumer is likely to mistakenly believe it is connected with that location. SAN ANTONIO SALSA, for example, would be deceptively misdescriptive, and therefore unregistrable, if it is actually made in New York City and not San Antonio.

Deceptive Marks

The USPTO will not register any mark it determines to be materially deceptive. A mark is materially deceptive if (a) it falsely describes the good or services, or their origin, and (b) the deception is likely to influence a consumer's purchasing decision. A materially deceptive mark cannot be registered even if it has acquired secondary meaning.

Disparaging Marks

The Lanham Act purports to prohibit the registration of any mark that disparages (i.e., brings into disrepute or contempt) any living or dead person, institution, belief or national symbol. In *Matal v. Tam*,[25] the Asian American band, The Slants, sought to register their band name as a trademark. The USPTO refused registration on the basis that it disparaged Asian American people. The U.S. Supreme Court reversed, holding that registered trademarks are private speech, not government speech. As such, they are protected by the First Amendment. The prohibition against registering "disparaging" trademarks violates the First Amendment right of freedom of speech.

Immoral or Scandalous Marks

Federal registration may be denied to a mark that is "immoral" or "scandalous."[26] The USPTO and courts have defined these terms in a variety of ways, such as "shocking to the sense of propriety, offensive to the conscience or moral feelings or calling out for condemnation" or "vulgar" or "lacking in taste, indelicate, morally crude." Profanity, depictions and references to sexual organs and acts, and sometimes nudity, often fall into the category of "scandalous or immoral."

The continuing validity of the Lanham Act's prohibition against the registration of immoral or scandalous content is uncertain, in view of the U.S. Supreme Court's ruling in *Tam*.

---

[25] 582 U.S. ____, 137 S. Ct. 1744 (2017).

[26] 15 U.S.C. § 1052 (2017).

TITLE OF A SINGLE BOOK OR MOVIE

The title of a single book or movie generally cannot be registered as a trademark. It may be possible to register a trademark in a recurring word or phrase that appears in every title in a series, though. In that situation, the public may associate the title with the same source.

Registration disclaimers

It is possible to register a mark without receiving the benefits of trademark registration for every aspect or element of it. This can happen either by omitting a particular claim or by disclaiming trademark rights in a particular aspect or element of a mark. Appropriate disclaimers in a registration application sometimes help prevent denials or delays.

Categories of goods and services

The categories of goods and/or services for which trademark protection is sought must be specified. There may be more than one, and both goods and services may be specified on the same application. The application must adequately describe them. The USPTO's *Acceptable Identification of Goods and Services Manual* lists acceptable identifications of goods and services.

Drawing

Every application must include an image or depiction of the mark. The USPTO calls all such images and depictions "drawings" even when the mark consists entirely of typewritten text. The drawing will become part of the USPTO's searchable database. It will also be published in the Official Gazette and will appear on the registration certificate.

Specimen of use

At least one specimen of use is required. It should exhibit the mark's actual use in commerce.

Filing fees

The filing fee for an application varies depending on the type of application—paper, TEAS, TEAS RF (reduced fee) or TEAS Plus—and the number of International Classes of goods or services selected. Current fees are posted at www.uspto.gov.

Examination

An examining attorney will review the application using the TMEP, search the USPTO database of existing registrations and applications, and decide whether it is registrable or not. The examination process can take months. The status of an application can be checked using the USPTO's Trademark Status and Document Retrieval system (TSDR) at www.uspto.gov.

Office actions

An office action is a communication from the USPTO in regard to a pending application. It may be a request for more information or it may be a notice of a deficiency or problem with the application. The time limit for responding to an office action is three months. An extension of time to respond may be requested.

An applicant who receives a final office action determining that the mark is not eligible for registration has three options:

- File a request for reconsideration
- Appeal to the TTAB
- Abandon the application.

The USPTO may consider an application abandoned if the applicant fails to timely respond to an office action. If that happens, a petition for reactivation may be filed with the Commissioner for Trademarks. The petition must be filed within sixty days. If the application is not reactivated, then it will be necessary to start the application process over from scratch, paying the filing fee again.

A denial of registration is not a determination that the applicant has no trademark rights. A common law trademark may exist even if the USPTO refuses to register it. Similarly, abandoning a registration is not the same thing as abandoning the mark itself.

Appeals

An appeal of an examiner's decision to the TTAB is called an *ex parte proceeding*. A TTAB decision may be appealed to the Court of Appeals for the Federal Circuit.

Publication for opposition

If the application for registration of the mark survives the examining attorney's examination, it will be published in the USPTO's *Official Gazette*. The purpose of publication is to give members of the public (including those with competing claims to the same mark) an opportunity to object to the registration.

Opposition proceedings

Anyone who believes registration may damage her interests may object to it by filing an opposition with the TTAB. The deadline for filing an opposition is thirty days from the date of first publication in the *Official Gazette*, unless an extension is requested and granted. An opposition initiates a legal proceeding. TTAB decisions in opposition proceedings may be appealed to the Federal Circuit Court of Appeals.

Notice of allowance

If the application for registration survives the examination process and opposition proceedings (if any), then the USPTO will issue a Notice of Allowance.

Certificate of registration

In the case of an application based on use, the USPTO will issue a registration certificate shortly after the Notice of Allowance is sent. The registration certificate for an intent-to-use application will be issued only after a proper and timely Statement of Use and specimen(s) are received in the USPTO office.

Cancellation of registration

The USPTO and others may file a petition to cancel a registration.

Under the recently enacted Trademark Modernization Act, anyone can file a petition to cancel a trademark registration alleging the registrant's non-use of the mark. The petition may be filed anonymously. Once a petitioner submits a prima facie case of non-use, the burden shifts to the registrant to establish use.

In addition, any person may file an *expungement* petition requesting cancellation of a registration on the basis that the mark has never been used in commerce on or in connection with some or all of the goods or services listed in the registration.

Any person may initiate a *reexamination* proceeding by filing a request to cancel a registration on the basis that the mark was not in use in commerce on or before the filing date of the application (or, in the case of an intent-to-use application, the deadline to file a statement of use).

Unlike a petition for cancellation on the grounds of abandonment, proof of the registrant's intent not to resume use is not necessary.

A person who fails to successfully challenge a registration in expungement or reexamination proceedings may still initiate a cancellation proceeding later.

Renewal and maintenance of registration

The term of a registration is ten years. It may be renewed for additional ten-year terms any number of times. In addition, the registrant must file an Affidavit of Use or Excusable Nonuse (also called a "Section 8 affidavit") between the fifth and sixth years of the first term. A filing fee is required. Failure to timely and properly file an Affidavit of Use or Excusable Nonuse, or to remit the filing fee, may result in cancellation of the registration before the end of the first term.

In rare cases, failure to use a mark may be excused if it is clear from the circumstances that the nonuse was not due to an intention to abandon the mark. A lack of consumer demand for the product or service is not an acceptable excuse for nonuse. The USPTO construes excusable nonuse very narrowly. Nevertheless, a trademark owner who has a good excuse for failing to use a mark should so indicate on the Declaration of Continued Use or Excusable Nonuse.

Between the ninth and tenth years after registration, another Affidavit of Use or Excusable Nonuse must be filed, this time along with an Application for Renewal. This must be done between every ninth and tenth year after the registration date thereafter. Again, failure to timely file and pay the filing fee may result in cancellation of the registration.

The USPTO will accept a late filing of one of these documents for up to six months after the applicable deadline, but an additional fee must be paid.

If, after the fifth year of registration on the Principal Register, there are no adverse decisions or pending proceedings involving the mark, and it has been in continuous use during that time, the registrant may file a Declaration of Incontestability (also called a "Section 15 declaration"), along with the applicable filing fee. This has the effect of removing some, but not all, grounds for cancellation of registration. Although not a mandatory filing, a Section 15 Declaration can be useful because it makes the rebuttable presumptions of ownership, validity, registration and exclusive right to use irrebuttable.

A Section 15 Declaration does not make a registered trademark absolutely incontestable. There are some exceptions. The following claims and defenses may still be asserted even if a Section 15 Declaration has been filed:

- The mark is (or has become) generic
- The mark is functional
- A prior registration is confusingly similar
- The owner has abandoned the mark
- Fraud in the procurement of the registration
- Fraud in the maintenance of the registration
- Use of the trademark to violate antitrust laws
- Prior use of a common law trademark
- Fair use
- Equitable defenses (e.g., laches, unclean hands)

®, ™ and ℠

The use of trademark symbols is governed by the law of the country in which a mark is used. In the United States, the encircled-R symbol—®—may be used only if the mark is federally registered. It is illegal to use this symbol on anything but a federally registered mark. Further, the mark may be used only in connection with the categories of goods and services listed in the registration. An applicant for federal registration does not acquire a right to use the ® symbol until the registration process is complete. Use of the ® symbol must be discontinued if a registered mark is no longer "live" because the registration has been canceled or abandoned. Unauthorized use of the ® symbol not only violates federal trademark laws; it may also constitute false advertising. In addition, an applicant's use of the symbol while an application for registration is still pending may result in a denial of registration.

The ™ symbol may be used for common law trademarks as well as registered ones. It may be used even if the USPTO has refused registration of the mark, provided that doing so does not violate false advertising or unfair competition laws. The ℠ symbol may be used for service marks.

Use of a trademark symbol is not absolutely necessary. It is highly recommended, though, for several reasons. Most important, it helps identify the mark as a trademark, not just a generic name for the product. Affixing a trademark symbol is not guaranteed to prevent genericide, but it can help. A trademark symbol also puts competitors on notice that someone is claiming an exclusive right to use the mark. This can discourage them from using an identical or confusingly similar term in connection with the same, similar or related goods or services. This is important in terms of preserving a mark's distinctiveness.

The owner of a registered mark continues to have an exclusive right to use the mark even if he fails to affix the ® symbol. Infringement of a registered mark to which the symbol has not been affixed is still unlawful. In some cases, though, the owner's remedies may be limited if he has not consistently used the ® symbol in connection with the mark.

Multinational trademarks

The geographic scope of a trademark normally is limited to the boundaries of the country in which the mark is legally enforceable as a trademark. In some countries, this means that only marks that are registered in the country are enforceable there. In other countries, it means that only marks that have been used in commerce in the country are enforceable there. The use or registration of a mark in one country does not create any trademark rights in other countries. Registration, too, is only national in scope. For this reason, it is normally either necessary or recommended to file an application for registration in each country in which trademark rights are or may be sought to be enforced.

Registration of foreign marks in the United States

If a trademark is registered in a foreign country, it may be registered in the United States on the basis of either use in commerce in the United States or foreign registration. A mark that is already registered in a foreign country may be registered in the United States even if it is not being used in the United States, provided the foreign registration is specified in the application as the filing basis. Like an intent-to-use application, the application must contain a statement of bona fide intent to use it. Unlike an intent-to-use application, U.S. registration of a mark registered in a foreign country may be issued before proof of use in the United States is furnished. If a foreign registrant fails to use the mark in the United States within a reasonable time after registration in the United States, however, the USPTO may cancel the registration on the basis of abandonment. A presumption of abandonment arises if the registrant fails to use the mark in the United States within three years after the registration in the United States. Abandonment may be found to have occurred sooner if there is evidence that the registrant has no intent to use the mark in the United States.

An application for registration of a foreign trademark is also known as a Section 66(a) registration, or a "registration for extension of protection." Section 66(a) is the provision of the Trademark Act dealing with the extension of the protection afforded by an international trademark to the United States pursuant to a treaty called the Madrid Protocol.

International registration

Unfortunately, three is not yet any system in place for the registration of a trademark that will be enforceable anywhere in the world. The Madrid Protocol makes it much easier to apply to register trademarks in multiple countries at one time, though. Pursuant to the Madrid Protocol, an applicant for a national registration may designate on the application any additional countries in which registration is desired, so long as those countries are members of the Madrid Protocol. This kind of registration is known as an *international registration.*

In the United States, this can all be done through the USPTO, thereby obviating the need to file separate applications with the trademark offices of each foreign country in which registration is desired. The USPTO takes care of forwarding the applications to the International Bureau of WIPO. The International Bureau then sends a request for extension of protection to each national office designated in the application.

Each individual country determines whether or not protection for a mark will be granted. The fact that registration has been granted in one country does not mean that another country must approve registration of the mark there. If the trademark office in a designated country does approves a request for extension of protection, though, then the mark is protected in that country to the same extent it would be if it had been registered in that country directly.

The European Union offers a *Community trademark*. A Community trademark extends protection for a mark to all countries that are members of the EU.

The owner of an international registration must meet the maintenance requirements for the international registration as well as for each of the countries in which the mark is registered or to which the protection of registration has been extended. For a mark registered in a foreign country as to which the protection of an international registration has been extended to the United States, the owner not only must satisfy U.S. requirements for maintaining registrations (continuing use declarations and renewals), but also must satisfy the requirements for maintaining the international registration and the registrations in the other countries where the mark is registered.

Recordation

Recordation of a trademark assignment means filing a record of it with the appropriate government office, i.e., the USPTO, a foreign country's and/or a state's designated office for trademark registrations and recordation.

Recording assignments of federally registered marks with the USPTO is recommended but not required. Failure to record an assignment with the USPTO does not affect the validity of the transfer. An unrecorded assignment still has the effect of transferring all rights in the mark to the assignee.

An unrecorded assignment of a federally registered mark is void as against a subsequent bona fide purchaser who had no knowledge or notice that the mark had already been assigned to someone else. A properly recorded assignment of a federally registered mark is not void as against a subsequent purchaser of the same mark.

To be valid as against a subsequent purchaser, a federal recordation must occur within three months of the assignment or prior to the subsequent purchase.

Proper federal recordation creates a rebuttable presumption that the assignment is valid.

4 PATENTS

Two distinguishing features of patents:

(1) They protect the exclusive right of inventors to commercially exploit their inventions.
(2) They do not arise by operation of law; it is necessary to apply to the federal government for one.

A patent is a grant of an exclusive right to market an invention for a defined period of time. It does not come into existence unless and until a governmental body issues one. It is a kind of property and may be transferred or licensed to others. In the United States, the federal government has exclusive jurisdiction to issue and regulate patents, and that power is vested in the U.S. Patent and Trademark Office (USPTO).

Kinds of patents

- Utility
- Design
- Plant.

Utility patents

About 90% of patents are utility patents. There are four kinds:

- machines
- human-made products
- compositions of matter
- processes.

Method patents, including business method patents, are a kind of process patent.

The bar for usefulness is not very high. The invention does not have to be an improvement over existing art or even commercially feasible. It merely needs to be operative and serve something other than an ornamental purpose.

BUSINESS METHODS

Historically, courts held that business methods were not patentable. This is still the rule in many countries, but it is no longer true in the United States. In 1998 the Federal Circuit Court of Appeals held, in *State Street Bank & Trust v. Signature Financial Group*,[27] that business methods are indeed capable of being patented, provided they meet all of the eligibility requirements (novelty, etc.). The U.S. Supreme Court affirmed this principle in *Bilski v. Kappos.*[28]

A business method is patentable only if it produces a concrete, tangible result. If it is not tied to a machine or the transformation of an article, it runs the risk of being an unpatentable abstract idea. In *Bilski*, the Court ruled that the claimed invention really just amounted to using mathematical formulae to apply the concept of hedging against the financial risk of price fluctuations to energy markets. As such, it was an abstract idea; hence, not patentable. As clarified later in *Alice Corporation v. CLS Bank International*[29] business method patentability requires a two-step analysis: (1) Does it involve an abstract idea? (2) If so, does it add something inventive to it, i.e., some

27 149 F.3d 1368 (Fed. Cir. 1998).

28 561 U.S. 593 (2010).

29 573 U.S. 208 (2014).

"new and useful end" that is not itself merely an abstract idea? The "new and useful end" must meet the non-obviousness requirement.

COMPUTER SOFTWARE

Algorithms and mathematical formulae are not patentable per se. An invention is not unpatentable merely because it contains an algorithm, though. A process synthesizing computer software or code with business methodologies or techniques may be patentable as a business method patent.

Following the decisions in *Bilski* and *Alice*, enforcing patents on online business method patents can be difficult. In addition to the "abstract idea" problem, the novelty and non-obviousness requirements can sometimes present obstacles. In one case, Soverain Software attempted to enforce patents it had obtained on online shopping cart programs. One of the companies it sued, Newegg, Inc., presented evidence of CompuServe's use of very similar shopping cart technology before Soverain secured its patents. This helped demonstrate that Soverain's shopping cart patents did not satisfy the non-obviousness requirement for patentability.[30]

In addition, some business method patents have expired. For example, the patent on Amazon.com's one-click shopping cart method, which allows customers to order online using predefined credit card and shipping address information fields rather than having to reenter this information each time, expired in 2017.

Design patents

Design patents are granted for the protection of nonutilitarian aspects of the design of an article of manufacture. They, too, must meet the requirements of novelty, originality, and non-obviousness. In addition, the design must be embodied in an article of manufacture and must be ornamental. A design patent will not be issued for a design that serves a non-ornamental purpose. New computer-generated icons and fonts are examples of designs that might qualify for design patent protection.

---

[30] Soverain Software LLC v. Newegg Inc. 705 F.3d 1333 (Fed. Cir. 2013).

Plant patents

A plant patent is for the protection of inventions or discoveries of new, asexually reproduced plant varieties other than tubers.

Requirements

Requirements for a patent are:

1) Protectable subject matter
2) Novelty
3) Non-obviousness
4) Usefulness
5) Enablement.

Protectable subject matter

Both deliberate creations and accidental discoveries are patentable.[31] In all cases, the invention or discovery must be a "useful process, machine, manufacture, or composition of matter, or any new and useful improvement thereof."[32] At least a modicum of human ingenuity or experimentation is required.

Examples of things that are *not* patentable:

- Natural laws
- Naturally occurring phenomena
- Abstract ideas (such as a principle of mathematics)
- Expressive elements of an invention.

Computer programs are sometimes patentable.

With the exception of design patents, the expressive elements of an invention are not protected by patent law. To the extent expression is merged with an idea, the idea is protected, if at all, only by patent law, not copyright law.

---

[31] 35 U.S.C. § 100
[32] 35 U.S.C. § 101

Novelty

To be patentable, an invention must be something new, i.e., original and unique. It must not already be in public use. To receive a U.S. patent, an invention must not be known or used by others in the United States, or patented or described in a printed publication in any country, at the time the applicant created it. A use in the United States by a person who concealed, suppressed or abandoned the technology does not count, however.

Merely maintaining the invention as a trade secret does not necessarily amount to "concealing, suppressing or abandoning" the invention, where the inventor actively and openly exploits the invention commercially.[33]

Non-obviousness

A patent will not be granted for relatively minor modifications of existing inventions that would be obvious to a person having ordinary skills in the relevant field.

Usefulness

Enablement

A patent will not be granted unless the application describes the invention in sufficient detail to enable a person to actually practice it. If the invention is a machine, then it must be possible for a person to actually build the machine using the description provided in the application. If the invention is a method, then there must be sufficient detail to enable a person to actually use the method.

Employee rights

A patent application is normally to be filed by the inventor. Unlike copyrights, where a work created by an employee for an employer is a work made for hire as to which the employer is deemed the author, an employee who creates an invention in the course of the employment normally continues to be considered the inventor despite the existence

[33] Dunlop Holdings, Ltd. v. Ram Golf Corp., 524 F.2d 33 (7th Cir. 1975).

of the employment relationship. An employer acquires rights in an employee's invention only if the employer either instructed the employee to create the specific invention in question or has entered into an assignment agreement with the employee. Contracts providing that all of an employee's legal rights for any invention created or discovered in the course of employment are automatically assigned to the employer are generally enforceable.

Even if the inventor has assigned away rights, however, the actual inventor must still be joined in the patent application.

The application

Unlike other kinds of intellectual property, a patent comes into being only by means of a grant from a government. In the United States, the application for such a grant must provide, along with other information, a description (called a "specification") of the invention. It must be sufficiently detailed to enable any person skilled in the art to make and use it. The specification must also explain how the invention differs from existing ones similar to it.

The application must also include a "claims" section describing the aspects of the invention for which a claim of patent protection is being made.

The application must be accompanied by a drawing of the invention, which can include a flow chart, schematic diagram or other methods of exemplifying the process or method sought to be patented.

The application must disclose any known and relevant prior art, and must also include an oath or declaration that the applicant is the first inventor of the invention. A nonrefundable filing fee must be paid.

The application will be assigned to a patent examiner, who will search prior art to determine the novelty and non-obviousness of the invention. If the examiner determines it is patentable, a patent will be granted and another fee must be paid. If the examiner denies the application, the applicant may either resubmit the application with changes that the applicant believes will make the invention patentable, or appeal the decision to the USPTO's Board of Appeals. Further appeal is to the federal court.

A patent application may be denied if the applicant intentionally misrepresents a material fact or fails to disclose known relevant prior art to the USPTO.

The application and examination process together are called *prosecution* of the patent. Patent prosecutions take varying amounts of time, but average about eighteen months.

American Inventors Protection Act

The American Inventors Protection Act[34] gives the USPTO power to regulate invention promoters, i.e., those who charge inventors money to secure patents for them. The AIPA establishes a "bill of rights" for inventors, and imposes fines and penalties on invention promoters who violate those rights. It also establishes a timeline for patent review, and enhances the ability of patent applicants to challenge administrative denials of their applications.

Duration

The term of utility and plant patents is 20 years from the date the application was filed. The term of a design patent is 14 years. Periodic maintenance fees must be paid in order to keep a patent in force.

Infringement

A patent gives the owner of the patent the exclusive right to exploit the invention within the jurisdiction that issued it. Infringement occurs when a person (including a business entity) makes, uses, sells, offers to sell, or imports a patented invention without authority to do so. Neither knowledge nor intent to infringe need be proven in order to prevail on a patent infringement claim. People have a duty to investigate to determine whether an invention is patented before exploiting it

There are two kinds of patent infringement: literal and equivalence. *Literal infringement* occurs when someone makes an unauthorized use of the exact same patented invention. Literal infringement occurs if all elements of a patented claim are used, even if the infringer adds some new elements to it. It does not occur, however, if the alleged infringer omits one or more of the elements. *Equivalence infringement* occurs when, although not all elements of the patented invention are used,

[34] Pub. L. 106–113, § 4302, 113 Stat. 1501, 1501A–556 (codified as amended in scattered sections of 35 U.S.C.)

substantial equivalents of those elements are used. If an invention performs substantially the same function in substantially the same way as a patented invention, it may be found to be an infringement under the doctrine of equivalents.

A patent owner is not allowed the benefit of the doctrine of equivalents with respect to any element she was obliged to drop from her claim in order to get the USPTO to grant the patent. This principle is known as *file wrapper estoppel*.

Importing infringing goods into the United States is an act of infringement. Exporting infringing goods is not. Making infringing goods or conducting sales of them in the United States will qualify as infringement, though, even if the goods are made and sold for export. Exporting the components of an infringing product for manufacture abroad may result in indirect infringement liability.

Direct and indirect infringement

Infringement may be direct or indirect. A person incurs direct liability by personally performing the infringing act. *Indirect* liability refers to situations in which a person may be held liable for someone else's infringing act.

Indirect liability may arise either by: (a) actively inducing (aiding and abetting) another person's infringement, or (b) contributing to the infringement by selling:

> a component of a patented machine, manufacture, combination or composition, or a material or apparatus for use in practicing a patented process, constituting a material part of the invention, knowing the same to be especially made or especially adapted for use in an infringement of such patent, and not a staple article or commodity of commerce suitable for substantial non-infringing use....[35]

Designing an infringing device which another person then manufactures is an example of "active inducement." Supplying a device or part that could be put to both infringing and non-infringing uses may also constitute active inducement, if the supplier promotes, through advertising or otherwise, the infringing use.

---

[35] 35 U.S.C. § 271(c) (2017).

Selling access codes, keys, passwords or other things that allow unauthorized persons to use and/or copy patented software is an example of an activity that might result in liability for contributory patent infringement.

Contributory liability will not attach unless: (a) the person knows the invention is patented, and (b) the person knows that use of the supplied component will constitute infringement.

Remedies

Both injunctive relief and monetary damages are available.

Injunctive relief may include both a preliminary injunction and a permanent injunction. To qualify for a permanent injunction, the patentee must establish four things, in addition to patent ownership:

(a) The patentee has suffered irreparable injury due to the infringement;
(b) Money damages ("the remedy at law") are not adequate;
(c) The balance of hardships favors the patentee;
(d) The public interest would not be harmed by the issuance of an injunction.

A patentee who is not able to prove lost profits may recover a reasonable royalty instead.

In exceptional cases of willful infringement, treble damages may be awarded.

The prevailing party may sometimes recover attorney fees, at least if the infringement was willful or if the other party engaged in inequitable conduct or bad faith litigation.

Statute of limitations

The statute of limitations for patent infringement is six years.

5 TRADE SECRETS

Although ideas and information such as recipes, formulas, customer lists, etc. do not get copyright protection, it may be possible to acquire exclusive rights in them if they qualify as trade secrets.

Both federal and state laws protect trade secrets. Nearly every state has enacted the Uniform Trade Secret Act (UTSA). It codifies much of the common law of trade secrets and makes some additions to it.

While laws vary in their particulars, the general principle set forth in all of them is that it is unlawful to misappropriate another person's trade secret, and doing so may result in liability for damages.

Requirements

A trade secret can be any kind of information – a formula, recipe, plan, design, pattern, data compilation, customer list, customer purchasing history, supplier list, financial data, marketing data, personnel information, physical device, method, process, device, computer software, new product ideas, new product launch date, price bids, specifications for how to build or operate a device or service, know-how related to a business, etc.—provided all of the following elements are present:

- It is secret;
- Reasonable measures to maintain secrecy;
- Commercial value of secrecy.

Secrecy

To qualify as secret, the information must be:

a) Not generally known; and
b) Not readily ascertainable by a person who can obtain economic value from its disclosure or use (such as a business competitor).

Information may be disqualified from trade secret protection if it is known by members of a particular industry, even if it is not known to the public at large.

A person who misappropriates a trade secret may remain liable for it even if the information later becomes generally known. The fact that information becomes generally known as a result of a person's act of misappropriation does not negate its status as a trade secret at the time the person misappropriated it. If the rule were otherwise, then people would be permitted to benefit from their own wrongdoing.

Information may be disqualified from trade secret status if it is readily ascertainable by someone who can derive economic value from its disclosure or use, whether or not evidence of actual knowledge exists. Thus, publication of the information in a trade journal, reference materials and the like will disqualify information from trade secret protection. Similarly, information that can be easily obtained through reverse engineering of publicly accessible software is disqualified from trade secret protection. The easier the information is to copy or acquire, the less likely it is to receive trade secret protection.

Reasonable measures to maintain secrecy

Reasonable precautions must be taken to protect a trade secret from being accessed or disclosed. This includes physical, procedural, and technical measures.

Storing a secret formula in a locked safe is an example of a physical measure. Marking a document as "confidential" or "secret" is another example.

Procedural measures are things like requiring employees to sign nondisclosure and noncompete agreements; restricting certain information to only those employees who have a need to know it in order to perform their jobs; non-solicitation agreements; and nondisclosure agreements with customers, clients, business partners, associates, contractors, consultants, and investors.

Technical measures include things like encryption, requiring a password to access a database, and the like.

It is not necessary to take every conceivable precaution to protect secrecy. Only "reasonable" measures are required. A court will not require a person to incur significant financial costs as a condition of receiving trade secret protection.[36]

Commercial value of secrecy

Normally, the commercial value of a trade secret is that it gives a business a competitive advantage. In determining whether information has commercial value, courts may consider the amount of money and effort expended to acquire or develop the information and the amount of money and time it would take for others to acquire or duplicate the information, along with any other evidence of value to a competitor. Merely keeping information about the company secret is not enough. For example, confidential information about a company's financial standing will not qualify as a trade secret unless there is evidence to show that this information is valuable to a competitor.

---

[36] E.I. du Pont de Nemours, Inc. v. Christopher, 431 F.2d 1012 (5th Cir. 1970).

Programming code may be a trade secret if it has economic value and reasonable efforts have been made to maintain its secrecy. Measures that computer software creators and vendors sometimes employ to protect trade secrets include: nondisclosure covenants in the licensing agreement; nondisclosure covenants with developers and testers; distribution only in executable form; and various kinds of security measures to prevent access to the source code. There have been cases where software licensors have lost trade secret protection by failing to include a nondisclosure covenant in the license agreement, where the licensor had done nothing to prevent customers from accessing the programming code.

Unlike noncompete agreements, nondisclosure agreements do not need to be limited to a short period of time. In fact, a nondisclosure agreement that is limited to a short period will undermine a company's claim of having taken "reasonable measures" to protect a trade secret. In one case, for example, a court held that a nondisclosure agreement that only required nondisclosure for a ten-year period was not a reasonable measure to protect a trade secret.

Patent vs. trade secret

Patent law complements trade secret law; it does not preempt it. An invention may be protected as a trade secret whether it is patentable or not. Inventors may rely on the protections of trade secret law while a patent application is being processed, provided it remains secret during that time. When a patent is issued, however, the invention can no longer receive protection as a trade secret. The disclosures that must be made in order to obtain a patent make the information "readily ascertainable" to others. Because the secrecy of an invention can give a company a competitive advantage of potentially unlimited duration, a company may prefer to maintain it as a trade secret rather than seeking patent protection for it. There is a risk to this approach, however: Another person or business could come up with the same idea independently and patent it. Of course, if the second company does not create the invention independently—if it misappropriates the first company's trade secret—then it may be liable for misappropriation of a trade secret.

Duration

Unlike patents, legal protection for a trade secret is of potentially indefinite duration. It will lose its protection as a trade secret, however, if it becomes generally known or become readily ascertainable by a person who can obtain economic value from it.

Misappropriation

Liability for misappropriation of a trade secret can arise in three ways:

- Obtaining it by improper means;
- Acquiring, disclosing or using it with knowledge or reason to know it was improperly obtained; or
- Disclosing or using it without consent, with knowledge or reason to know that it was acquired under circumstances giving rise to a duty to maintain its secrecy.

Some examples of "improper means":

- Theft
- Bribery
- Fraud
- Electronic espionage
- Breach of a nondisclosure agreement
- Inducement to breach a nondisclosure agreement
- Violation of a statutory prohibition.

Since the Computer Fraud and Abuse Act prohibits accessing a computer without permission, obtaining a trade secret this way would be improper. Violating the Electronic Communications Privacy Act by intercepting an email message would be another example. These are not the only examples that could be given.

Independently creating or developing information that happens to be the subject of another person's trade secret is not improper.

Accessing publicly available information also is not improper.

Consent, express or implied, is a defense. Expiration of the statute of limitations is also a defense. The UTSA provides for a three-year limitations period. Some states have specified lengthier limitations periods, such as five years. Limitations periods generally are measured from the date the plaintiff discovered (or reasonably should have discovered) the misappropriation.

Of course, if a person misappropriates a trade secret in a way that is prohibited in a contract, then there may be liability for breach of contract as well as misappropriation of a trade secret.

Crimes

Unauthorized use or disclosure of a trade secret may also be a crime. The Economic Espionage Act[37] makes the theft or appropriation of a trade secret by fraud, artifice or deception, with intent to harm, or with knowledge that it will cause harm (including financial loss) to its owner or will benefit a foreign government, a federal crime. A violation is punishable by a fine of up to $5,000,000 and up to ten years imprisonment. If done with knowledge or intent to benefit a foreign government, it is punishable by a fine of up to $10,000,000 and fifteen years imprisonment. The Act also provides for civil penalties.

For purposes of the Act, "appropriating" a trade secret means copying, duplicating, sketching, drawing, photographing, downloading, uploading, altering, destroying, replicating, transmitting, photocopying, delivering, sending, mailing, communicating, or conveying the secret without authorization.

---

[37] Economic Espionage Act of 1996, Pub. L. 104–294, 110 Stat. 3488 (codified at 18 U.S.C. § 1831)

Several states have also made the unauthorized acquisition, use or disclosure of a trade secret a crime.

Disclosure exemptions

There may be situations in which a business is legally required to disclose a trade secret to a government entity. Fortunately, there are sometimes steps that can be taken to prevent further disclosure to the public. Copyright regulations offer ways to submit required deposit copies (which normally are viewable by any member of the public at the Library of Congress) without disclosing trade secret information. FOIA rules giving the public a right to access to records maintained by government agencies contain some exceptions for trade secret material. Similar laws and regulations exist at the state and local level.

Documents filed in court generally may be viewed by the public. A business must take care, therefore, to ensure that pleadings and other documents filed with a court do not disclose a trade secret. The same is true of documents and information a party requests during the discovery phase of litigation. Under court rules and the Uniform Trade Secrets Act, a business may bring a motion to seal a record, or to hold a hearing in camera (without public access), and/or for a protective order.

Before submitting material containing a trade secret to a court, agency or other public entity, a business should carefully research and follow the entity's trade secret protection protocol.

6 OTHER KINDS OF INTELLECTUAL PROPERTY

Information

Federal copyright and patent laws preempt state misappropriations laws that conflict with, or regulate the same things as either of those federal laws do. Since copyright protects expression but not facts or information, states remain free to establish and enforce causes of action for misappropriation of information (provided the information in question is not a patented invention.) Thus, for example, a state may provide a remedy for breach of a contract to refrain from copying and distributing information.

Some states have gone further, providing a remedy for appropriation of information in circumstances amounting to unfair competition. *International News Service v. Associated Press*[38] is the leading case. In that case, one news service was "scooping" the other by accessing and publishing information the other one gathered before the service that gathered the information had a chance to publish it. The court held that the news service that had expended effort gathering the information could sue the other news service for appropriating the information to its own use in a way that prevented the first news service from exploiting it commercially. Although grounded in unfair

---

[38] 248 U.S. 215 (1918).

competition law, this "hot news" theory of liability has not been approved in all jurisdictions. Moreover, those that do recognize the cause of action are not in agreement about what must be proven in order to succeed on the claim.

State law causes of action for misappropriation of expressive content, of course, are preempted by the federal Copyright Act. Distinguishing between expression and information is not always easy, however. In *Barclay's Capital Inc. v. Theflyonthewall.com, Inc.*,[39] for example, a federal court held that a stock advisor's recommendations are expressive, not informational. Therefore, publishing them without permission could be a violation of copyright law, but could not be used as the basis for a state law misappropriation claim.

Although traditional common law has not allowed recovery for conversion of intangibles, some courts have begun to extend the tort of conversion to intangible property, too. For example, a New York court has held that electronic records are legally indistinguishable from paper versions of the same records for purposes of conversion law.[40] Of course, the other required elements of a conversion claim would then need to be alleged and proven.

Ideas

Copyright law does not protect ideas. Patent law only protects patentable inventions. Yet, there may be situations where it would be unfair to allow a person to profit from someone else's idea without compensating the originator of the idea in some way.

If an idea originator enters into a contract under which the idea exploiter is obliged to pay the idea originator for the idea, then the person who exploits the idea may be sued for breach of contract if she does not pay as agreed. Even in the absence of a written or oral agreement, a contract sometimes may be implied from the conduct of the parties, their course of dealing, and/or customary practices in the trade.

---

[39] 650 F. 3d 876 (2nd Cir. 2011).

[40] Thyroff v. National Mut. Ins. Co., 864 N.E.2d 1272 (N.Y. 2007).

In some situations, trade secret law might provide a remedy for stolen ideas. To receive protection as a trade secret, the idea must not be generally known at the time the originator of the idea alleges it somebody wrongfully appropriated it.

Some courts hold that idea cannot be protected as a trade secret unless it has acquired value through use.

In the absence of a viable breach of contract or trade secret claim, resort must be made to common law theories of liability for stealing someone's idea. At one time, these included conversion (which treats an idea as a kind of property); unjust enrichment (quasi-contract); unfair competition; misappropriation of confidential information; fraud (in obtaining access to the secret); interference with prospective business advantage; or breach of fiduciary duty. Note that the Uniform Trade Secrets Act contains a provision stating that the Act displaces equivalent common law causes of action. Most, but not all, states have enacted this provision. In those states that have enacted this provision, claims for conversion, misappropriation of confidential information, unjust enrichment, unfair competition, fraudulently obtaining access to a trade secret, and interference with prospective business advantage are no longer permitted if the interest sought to be vindicated is the same kind of interest that trade secret law protects.

The Uniform Trade Secrets Act does not displace common law claims for breach of contract. Fiduciary duties, including a duty of loyalty, are implied as a matter of law in certain kinds of relationships. Employees owe fiduciary duties to their employers; agents, to their principals; trustees to the beneficiaries; directors and officers, to the corporation; partners, to each other. Courts are not in agreement about the extent to which the Uniform Trade Secrets Act displaces common law claims for breach of fiduciary duty. The trend, however, is to hold that the Act does not supersede common law causes of action for breach of fiduciary duty except to the extent the cause of action is the equivalent of a cause of action for misappropriation of a trade secret.

Defenses to misappropriation of an idea depend on the theory of liability that is advanced. In every kind of case, however, independent development of the idea is a defense. A person who develops an idea independently, without knowledge that someone else had the same idea, would not be misappropriating anything. This is why some companies segregate mail containing unsolicited ideas to prevent their product developers and marketers from having access to them.

Unless it qualifies as a misappropriation of a trade secret, breach of a contractual or fiduciary obligation, or patent or copyright infringement, a cause of action for "stealing an idea" may be difficult to sustain. Courts in a number of jurisdictions do not recognize a common law tort of misappropriation of an idea that does not fall into one of these categories. An argument could be made that a claim of an exclusive right to exploit an idea on the sole basis that it is novel—that is, a claim to an idea that is not grounded in contract, fiduciary duty, copyright, trademark or trade secret law—is preempted by federal patent law.

According to the Restatement (3d) of Unfair Competition:

> [N]o general rule of law prohibits the appropriation of a competitor's ideas, innovations, or other intangible assets once they become publicly known. In addition, the federal patent and copyright statutes now preempt a considerable portion of the domain in which the common law tort might otherwise apply. The better approach, and the one most likely to achieve an appropriate balance between the competing interests, does not recognize a residual common law tort of misappropriation.[41]

The Restatement's position is that recovery for misappropriation of an idea should be allowed only in the following cases:

- Trade secret;
- Breach of contract (express or implied); or
- Violation of an intellectual property statute (e.g., the Copyright Act or the Patent Act)

---

[41] Restatement (3d) Unfair Competition 38, comment b (1995).

Visual artists' rights of attribution and integrity

European laws have long protected the "moral rights" of visual artists. Since December 1, 1990, the Visual Artists Rights Act[42] protects the moral rights of visual artists in the United States, too.

"Moral rights" legislation seeks to protect the reputations of visual artists by giving them rights of:

- Attribution
- Freedom from false attribution
- Integrity.

The right of *attribution* means the right to be identified as the creator of a particular work of art. It also includes the right to prevent works not created by an artist from being attributed to the artist.

The *integrity* right means the right to prevent the destruction, distortion, mutilation or other modification of a work, and to prevent the attribution of a mutilated or modified version of a work to the original artist.

Scope

The protections of the Visual Artists Rights Act extend only to certain kinds of works:

- Paintings
- Drawings
- Prints
- Sculptures
- Signed still photographs produced solely for exhibition.

---

[42] 17 U.S.C. § 106A.

The work must exist in only a single copy, or in a limited edition of no more than 200 copies that are signed and consecutively numbered by the author, or, in the case of a sculpture, in multiple cast, carved, or fabricated sculptures of 200 or fewer that are consecutively numbered by the author and bear the signature or other identifying mark of the author.

Only visual art is protected by the Act. In addition, the following kinds of works are specifically excluded from the protections of the Visual Artists Rights Act:

- posters (as distinguished from prints)
- maps
- globes
- technical drawings, diagrams, models
- applied art
- audiovisual works
- books, magazines, newspapers, periodicals
- electronic publications
- databases
- electronic information services
- advertising,
- promotional or merchandising items
- descriptive works, covering, or packaging materials or containers
- uncopyrighted works
- works made for hire.

A work that is not within the scope of protection of the Visual Artists Rights Act may nevertheless be protected by copyright, trademark or other law. A work must be protected by copyright, however, in order to receive the protections of the Visual Artists Rights Act.

Duration

For works created after December 1, 1990, the attribution and integrity rights in a work terminate at the end of the calendar year in which the artist dies. Such rights in collaborative works continue until the end of the calendar year in which the last surviving author dies.

For works created before December 1, 1990, the rights last as long as copyright does, but only if the artist was still the owner of title to the work (i.e., had not sold or otherwise transferred title to it) as of December 1, 1990.

Non-transferability

Visual Artists Rights Act rights ("moral rights") are not transferable. They are independent of copyright. An artist continues to have moral rights even after assigning the copyright to someone else. By the same token, mere ownership of the copyright does not give a person standing to enforce moral rights. Only the artwork creator enjoys these rights.

Waiver

To be enforceable, a waiver of an attribution or integrity right must:

- be in writing;
- be signed by the artist;
- expressly waive Visual Artists Rights Act rights;
- identify the work; and
- specify the uses of the work to which the waiver applies.

A waiver of Visual Artists Rights Act rights does not operate as a transfer of copyright in the work unless the agreement expressly provides that it does. A transfer of copyright, or a transfer of a copy in which a copyrighted work is embodied, does not operate as a waiver of Visual Artists Rights Act rights.

A waiver of Visual Rights Act rights by one coauthor waives them for all coauthors.

Semiconductor chips

The Semiconductor Chip Protection Act of 1984[43] protects the topography, the layout and design, of semiconductor chips. Protection is acquired by applying for "mask work" registration, accompanied by identifying material, and paying the required filing fee. The process is similar to copyright registration, but it is not the same thing.

The term "mask work" is not limited to actual masks used in chip manufacture but is broadly defined to include the topographic creation embodied in semiconductor masks and chips.

Reverse engineering is permitted.

Non-functionality requirement

Semiconductor chip protection does not extend to the functional aspects of a chip design. For that kind of protection, a patent would be needed.

Duration

Protection lasts for 10 years.

Infringement

Remedies for infringement are similar to those for copyright or patent infringement.

Vessel hull designs

Although designs are not protected by copyright, the Digital Millennium Copyright Act added copyright-like protections for vessel hull designs.[44]

---

[43] 17 U.S.C. §§ 901-914

[44] 17 U.S.C. §§ 1301 to 1332.

A "vessel" is any boat or other vehicle that is designed and capable of steering a course on or through water through its own means of propulsion, and that is capable of carrying and transporting one or more passengers. The hull is the frame or body of the vessel.

Protection for vessel hull designs lasts for ten years and is available only for original designs that are embodied in an actual vessel hull. No protection exists for designs that exist only in drawings or models.

ABOUT THE AUTHOR

Tom James is a copyright and trademark attorney. He is licensed to practice in Minnesota and admitted to the bars of the 8th and Federal Circuit Courts of Appeals and the United States Supreme Court. He is also authorized to represent clients in Copyright Claims Board (CCB) and Trademark Trials and Appeals Board (TTAB) proceedings. He writes the popular law blog, *The Cokato Copyright Attorney* and is the author of *E-Commerce Law* and *Website Law*.

www.ingramcontent.com/pod-product-compliance
Lightning Source LLC
LaVergne TN
LVHW022043200926
848481LV00003B/765
* 9 7 8 1 9 4 6 3 9 7 0 9 6 *